Praise for *Venice Rising: A*

Venice Rising is a compilation of eye witness reports from Venetians who have experienced unprecedented challenges. With honesty and wisdom they write of their fears, resilience, and hope. After sustaining devastating flood damage and loss of tourism, Venice has been returned to her residents. It is time that we listen to them.

--- JoAnn Locktov, Bella Figura Publications

**

I loved Venice at first sight, but it wasn't until I read *Venice Rising* that I truly appreciated — and fell in love with -- Venetians. They are, as historian William Thayer observed a century ago, "magnificent by nature."

In the last year Venice has reeled under two disasters: a devastating once-in-a-century flood and the coronavirus crisis that triggered a months-long lockdown. In *Venice Rising*, a mosaic of citizens — artisans, rowers, teachers, performers, shop owners, scions of its oldest families — present a first-hand view of their city as they had never seen it: deserted, silent, isolated, anxious yet at the same time never more beautiful or serene.

Venice Rising is a symphony of love, with many voices blending together to stir the soul just as deeply as their beloved hometown has for so many centuries.

--- Dianne Hales, author of *La Bella Lingua, La Passione,* and *Mona Lisa*

**

When Venice was at her most serenely beautiful, there was no one there to see her except the Venetians themselves. For ten terrifying, precious weeks, the Venetians got to know their city again.

In a city "naked without admirers," a city resting from overtourism, there emerge new thoughts for a more mindful future. This timely and moving book is expertly curated by Kathleen Ann González, author of *A Beautiful Woman in Venice*.

--- Michelle Lovric, author of *The Book of Human Skin, The Remedy,* and *Carnevale*

**

Whenever I start research for a book project, I always begin with primary sources—things written at the time. There's nothing quite like hearing the voices and reading the words of people who've lived in a certain place and time, especially if they've endured a traumatic collective experience like war, natural disaster, or disease. As a student of Venetian history, I'm gratified that Kathleen González has taken on the important task of capturing the firsthand stories of Venetians who've experienced the staggering challenges of 2019 and 2020 in their native city. In addition to giving hope to those of us who love Venice about the resilience of the city and of Venetians themselves, *Venice Rising* will also be an important source for those who want to understand our tumultuous times through the eyes of Venetians who experienced them.

—Laura Morelli, art historian and historical novelist

venice rising

AQUA GRANDA, PANDEMIC, REBIRTH

Edited by Kathleen Ann González

Ca' Specchio
San Jose
2020

© Copyright 2020 Kathleen Ann González
All rights reserved. No part of this publication may be reproduced without the prior permission in writing from the author, except for brief quotations used in reviews and articles.
Kathleen Ann González, 1965 –
Venice Rising: Aqua Granda, Pandemic, Rebirth
www.kathleenanngonzalez.com
Cover by RJ Wofford II
Cover photographs by Agostino Gargiulo, Marie Ohanesian Nardin, and Rosemary Wilmot; back cover photograph by Filippo Gaggia.
ISBN: 9798670068093
First Edition

Table of Contents

Preface: Kathleen Ann Gonzalez
Foreword: Rosemary Wilmot

1. Elena Almansi: "Frames"	1
2. Francesca Barozzi: "Empty Spaces and Magical Silence"	6
3. Piero Bellini: "Venice, Piazza San Marco, April 2020, Covid-19 Time, 02.00 a.m."	8
4. Mariangela Bognolo: "Venice, Queen of Strength and Beauty"	10
5. Manuela Brunello: "*L'Arazzo Vivente*"	14
6. Vera Brunello: "A Long Life to Venice!"	18
7. Manuel Carrión: "A Catalyst"	24
8. Monica Cesarato: "Venetian Soul"	31
9. Caterina Codato: "The Tank"	37
10. Jane Da Mosto, Eleonora Sovrani, and Kasia Ruszkowska: "We Are Here Venice: Novel Approaches to Awareness-Raising and Consensus-Building"	43
11. Romi Loch Davis: "Maybe Just Maybe"	51
12. Sigrid de Montrond: "Venice, A Cry from the Heart"	54
13. Gregory Dowling: "March 15, 2020"	56
14. Maria Gabriella Emiliani: "Lingering at the Window"	62
15. Filippo Gaggia: "In Slow Motion, Time Expands"	70
16. Chiara Gatta: "A Storm of Art, Colors, Story"	74
17. Graziella Giusto: "*35 Minuti e sono da Te*"	77
18. Lorenzo Gregolin: "Hymn to San Marco"	85
19. Catherine Kovesi: "V Is for Venice"	88
20. Iris Loredana: "The Yellow Rose of Venice"	92
21. Luana Segato Luse: "A Work with a Soul"	99
22. Alessia Manente: "In the Shadow of Manin"	102
23. Fernando Masone: "Exceptional Venice"	106
24. Marie Ohanesian Nardin: "Tragedy Guides Us to Change"	109
25. Liesl Odenweller: "Exploring the Silver Lining of Adversity"	117
26. Paolo Olbi: "*Non È Facile*" / "It's Not Easy"	124
27. Elena Grassi Orsoni: "*Vorrei Parlarti, Signore....*" / "I Would Like to Speak to You, Lord"	130

28. Barbara Pastor: "*Lettera ad Amici dell'Altra Parte del Mondo*" / "Letter to Friends on the Other Side of the World"   133
29. Alessandro Santini: "Splendor and Sadness"   138
30. Rachele Scarpa: "Like a Phoenix"   145
31. Giuliano Tonolo: "My Little Dream"   148

Acknowledgments   152
About the Editor   153

Preface

When a spectacular full double rainbow stretched its arc over Venice in April of 2020, people broke into joyous smiles and felt their hearts expand with hope. More than one friend in Venice sent me a photo of that rainbow, and even from as far away as California, I felt that rainbow's message enter my heart. I had followed the dark days of the November 2019 *aqua granda*, a Venetian term for the once-in-a-century flood, understanding its disastrous impact so similar to the 1966 high water. And then in the spring, as we learned more about the developing Covid-19 pandemic, my heart ached for the losses Venice was sustaining, the privations of its citizens, and my own sadness at canceling my annual summer visit. There would be for me no live music at the San Giacomo dell'Orio *sagra*, no gelato at Ca' d'Oro, no late night *giro*, no Redentore fireworks, no gliding gondola ride, no spritz with friends in the *campo*. My personal loss, though acute, was certainly dwarfed by the loss of liberties and health for Venetians and the loss to the city's businesses, craftspeople, and artistic life.

While compiling *First Spritz Is Free: Confessions of Venice Addicts*, I reveled in the contributors' paeans to Venice—their childhood memories, their joyful experiences, their swelling hearts full of love for this watery city. I thought that *First Spritz* might indeed be the first of a series of books, but I never could have anticipated the theme that arose for its sequel. When Rosemary Wilmot suggested collecting the stories of people who lived in Venice through the *aqua granda* and the pandemic, I initially envisioned a darker book, a book full of woe and loss and dismay. How can we contemplate a spritz with friends when the *osterie* are closed and everyone is masked? When people are unemployed, their houses and shops damaged, and they must stay apart for everyone's safety?

Alas, I underestimated these Venetians.

Venice has survived other plagues and floods and would survive this one, too.

I began receiving stories of disbelief at the wind's strength and tide's destruction, of areas so flooded that streets and canals became one, of hip boots and sirens. Then stories of looking longingly at empty *campi*, at endless days trapped indoors, at fear for the loss of traditional arts and the patrons who support them.

Each story started in this way but then turned—to hope. Hope for a fresh look at the tourism industry. Hope for gathering with friends once again. Hope for creating new ways to live together and support the arts and envision a Venice that could thrive anew. Some wrote of an almost mystical love or ethereal philosophy evoked by the dramatic events they have lived through. And all wrote with determination and new dreams.

The authors who have shared their writing with you do so for their love of Venice. All proceeds from the sale of this book will be donated to organizations that support Venetian culture, arts, and architecture: We are here Venice, No Grandi Navi, and Venice Calls, organizations born in Venice and run by locals. Many of the authors here are also traditional craftspeople or Venetian business owners themselves, and we hope that their stories inspire readers to learn more about Venice's unique arts and crafts to support a renaissance. You'll see most stories in English, often in translation from Italian, but a few stories are presented in Italian or in both languages. We present them in this way in hopes of sharing the most authentic voices and to honor the writers' wishes.

Venice Rising: Aqua Granda, Pandemic, Rebirth carries the promise of the rainbow, its hope for rebirth and its desire to create something better. A grassroots groundswell is going to remake Venice, and the stories and poems and conversations and letters and images herein will help us all to fulfill that covenant.

Kathleen Ann González
July 2020

Foreword By Rosemary Wilmot

In 2015 I first became aware of Kathleen González after finding her interview with Manuel Carrión, an artist on the Island of Giudecca in Venice. I read her books and just loved them. In 2018 after reading *First Spritz is Free: Confessions of Venice Addicts,* I was hooked on this style of writing; the chapters in this book by writers of all walks of life in Venice and beyond its shores were just amazing.

I wrote to Kathleen and asked her if she had any plans to publish another *Spritz* anthology, but at that point in time she had no plans to do so.

Since 2015 my husband Brian and I have made many good friends from Venice and the surrounding Veneto area. These friends have become very close to us as a family, and we have been very lucky spending time with them at their homes and having them come to London as well. We have been guests at the Redentore at the Esercito Militare, and to see inside this historical building was an honor. It is on the Riva degli Schiavoni with a ringside seat of the famous Redentore fireworks: the intense magic of the finale, which has to be seen to be believed, the power of the noise, and the exhilaration it produces.

We saw the Frecce Tricolori in Lido di Jesolo as guests of our friends, having great seats and watching this stunning display of color with the planes flying at speed over our heads performing mind-boggling feats and with the red, white, and green smoke of the Italian flag. The finale is spectacular—with opera playing so loud and the planes flying barely above our heads, it is Italy at its best.

We have seen the Regatta Storica from the boat of Row Venice, shouting and screaming for the girls from Row Venice to "Come on, hurry up!" The colors and pageantry are so different when seen from a boat. These friends also cared for me and cooked for me with love when I was ill.

It is wonderful to have made these friends, and this makes the whole experience of the *aqua granda* and pandemic so much more poignant. We feel such a deeper involvement because of them.

Fast forward to November 12, 2019. I became aware via Facebook that Venice was expecting a very high *acqua alta* and *scirocco* winds blowing at over 100 km an hour. Friends of ours who live in Venice were telling us of increasing problems with flooding, and the predictions from the Comune were rising higher and higher all the time. Apparently the sirens kept going, indicating a very big problem. I contacted Manuel Carrión after seeing a dreadful video of how badly Giudecca Island was flooding and could see he was going to have a very badly flooded studio. So you can see, this had a profound effect on many of our friends.

Knowing someone personally involved makes a huge difference to your understanding. I stayed up late that night writing to friends to see how they were. Some, of course, did not reply until the morning; some were writing at midnight and 1:00 a.m. after they had cleaned the best they could. Many of their voices are in here, and I am so happy to have them share their experiences.

But, in the tragedy came heartwarming stories. The university and schools were closed, but 1,500 students helped the residents of Venice with whatever they could. They rallied round them, putting their arms around them. My God, was that needed.

When in the new year Covid-19 struck and literally tore the economic heart out of Venice, this was a real tragedy of something never seen in our lifetime. It was destined to become a worldwide pandemic, which is still ongoing as I write. Friends who live there told us of the calm beauty that descended upon Venice; one told me this was how it was when she was a child: "A miracle of peace." The beauty of the water as it was not disturbed by the *vaporetti* and the motor boats stirring up the sludge, but photos of beauteous color were on Facebook, the pandemic bringing such peace and beauty amongst such terror of the virus itself. Is this ever going to end? And what will we be left with afterwards? All this news was scaring Venice and our friends. "Whatever will happen to us?" they asked.

This of course affected so many people in Venice. I was sitting at home one evening thinking about what I was seeing. Many people were writing their thoughts and feelings: first *aqua granda*, now Covid-19.... I was seeing heartbreaking and wonderful stories of people's lives and then I thought, "Kathleen, NOW is the time! We need to capture these stories, thoughts, and feelings while they are fresh in people's minds and hearts."

We are all living through history. Venice is unique in its *aqua granda,* but combined with a virus pandemic ... could this be the rebirth Venice is waiting for?

Kathleen loved the idea, and we started to gather wonderful essays for this project.

The stories are amazing and give us hope and inspiration. Readers, you are just going to love it. This book is heartwarming. Come on in and ENJOY!!

"Frames"
by Elena Almansi

"Closed due to illness." This is what Mario put up on his shutters. For the past 60 years, he has been managing a shop near Campo San Tomà, selling handmade frames and old posters.

It is February 23. Newspapers publish the first stories of the contagion in Italy. Gyms do not allow people in, even though outside thousands of people celebrate Carnevale.

March 8: The news of the beginning of the lockdown upsets the people of Venice, which was deemed to be a red zone.

Someone writes "Good luck" on Mario's sign.

Police forces are deployed all over the city to make sure that everyone stays home. People with dogs attract suspicion from the rest of the population, who think that maybe they are using the dog as an excuse to leave the house again and again.

Reclusion makes people bitter: mean comments can be heard from the windows, directed at every single person walking below them. "Look at that idiot," "What's he doing outside?!" and "Stay home!" Perhaps they don't know that the person they shouted at was a doctor coming home from his shift, or a shop assistant, or a *vaporetto* pilot.

It is bewildering to go from normality to reclusion; normality for me was being outdoors all the time, as my activities predominantly take place out in the fresh air. Usually I am training for my rowing races, teaching my students how to row in the Venetian way, and simply walking around to meet friends and drink a couple of beers or a Cynar spritz.

Initially we all thought that the lockdown would last no more than a week, so we all stayed strong and hung in there. We spent our days doing practically nothing, refusing to give in to the idea that it was going to be long-term.

But time went on and weeks passed, and the situation, rather than getting better, got worse: at home, we started to lose our minds.

Supermarkets are raided as if we are in wartime and as if it is necessary to stock up in order to survive. The queues outside supermarkets are never-ending. Home feels like a prison, and the "out-of-home" hour is spent queuing at the supermarket, and when you finally get in, almost all of what you need is already gone.

At that point you realize that many of your fellow citizens are at the end of their tether and show the first signs of breakdowns, just like you.

Browsing the web I see a Red Cross appeal: they're looking for people to deliver food to the elderly and all the particularly vulnerable people who are shielding and not allowed to leave the house.

I want to be useful, and I also want to get moving again: my legs, used to walking at least 10 kilometers every day, start to feel very heavy. I do some research and find out that the Red Cross is relying on small associations and local charities, because it was not easy for them to coordinate efforts in a city without cars and whose mobility is so different from anywhere else in the world.

Just like during the exceptional *aqua granda* last November, a large number of young Venetians got involved: they are the only ones who go around the city, with shopping bags and medicines, ringing people's doorbells.

April 1: The association Row Venice, of which I'm a member, decides to help as much as possible and do its bit. We are 20 female rowers and have four rowing boats, called *batele*. We begin to join forces with farmers to deliver door-to-door locally sourced fruit and vegetables. We apply for a permit from the Civil Protection agency, specifying that we are fully available to deliver everywhere in the city. Shortly after, we start to take out three rowing boats at the same time, also delivering meals cooked by restaurants that are still closed to the public. We row more than 13 kilometers a day in a city completely empty, without waves. The waves created by the passage of motor boats in the canals of Venice have been a long-debated problem, which is accentuated by the heavy traffic during tourist season. The frequent, high waves damage the ground floors of historical buildings and make it hard for rowing boats to circulate. Seeing the canals empty and smooth is surreal.

Never again will we witness the magic that Venice is showing us now, and we are deeply moved. We are used to managing our way through the waves, taking on water, shouting at those who don't pay attention to smaller boats, yet now we find ourselves in such perfect conditions for rowing. The ones receiving the goods are thrilled, and they praise our efforts. Deliveries have always been made by motor boat, and going back to the good old ways is an exciting change. Journalists from all over the world have come to Venice to cover our lockdown story. They see us rowing on boats full of vegetables and they ask for an interview. Our story is traveling around the world: the US, Indonesia, Norway, the UK, Germany, France .... We could not imagine that mere volunteering could become such a sensation. Perhaps, the fact that we are a group of female rowers in a city where this role has traditionally been a male one has contributed to turning our activity into an interesting piece of news.

May 4: The sign on Mario's door has been blown away in a day of *bora*, the mighty, cold wind coming from the north-east. His shop is still closed.

It is the beginning of the so-called "second phase" in Italy. After two months of deliveries, we can take stock of what we have achieved. We realize that not only have we helped individuals and businesses, but we have also come up with an idea for sustainable transport in Venice—respectful of the environment and the Lagoon—and we have shown its feasibility. By keeping track of our journeys with GPS, we noticed that our boats were exceeding the low speed limits imposed on motor boats within the city center to reduce high waves. This led us to think that rowing as a means of transport would actually be faster, as well as healthier and more sustainable.

End of May: Rowing clubs are reopening, and we can finally take our boats out and train for the regattas that may take place over the summer. We will continue our service volunteering until the businesses we are working for will have settled and got back to their activities as usual.

We are starting to work on a project to implement what should already be the norm: turning motor transport in the historical center into rowing transport, in order to preserve the environment and the city's traditions.

June 2: Tourists are back, and it looks like the whole of the Veneto is pouring into its capital city. Gondoliers can once again be seen along the canals with clients onboard, and we are starting to give rowing classes to residents of the city of Venice. We are receiving a high number of bookings, and we couldn't be happier.

Mario hasn't reopened yet. I ask Piero for news, as I am a little worried, and he tells me Mario is not sure he will open at all. After the *aqua granda* he has suffered quite a blow. All the wood he would use to make his frames was flooded. He hasn't had electricity in his shop for a while now, and he's been working with a flashlight on his head. Disheartened, he's taken some time off to think, but in the *campo* his presence is dearly missed.

June 12: For the first time since the start of the pandemic, we have given rowing classes to tourists. It feels like a rebirth. The local administration is making sure regattas will commence in July, and this too is great news.

Mario eventually reopened, and all the *campo* congratulated him with a heartfelt "We missed you."

"Back to the oars" then. Row Venice comes back to life, together with the rest of the city. We are aching, but we stand tall, as we always have.

Biography

Elena Almansi, also known as "Nena," is a Venetian female rower, born in 1992. After acquiring her diploma, unlike many of her peers who left the city to follow their path elsewhere, Elena found hers in her beloved city, Venice, in its roots and deepest traditions. She is a spokeswoman for women's rights in the field of sport. Nena has been a rowing instructor for over ten years at Row Venice, an association that promotes Venetian rowing in Venice and the world, teaching it to tourists and residents. Learn more at rowvenice.org.

"Empty Spaces and Magical Silence"
by Francesca Barozzi

This unique town, Venice, was built for a soft way of living and for silence.

This town—which for centuries everybody tried to define, to describe, and in spite of this nobody found its true deep meaning—this town finally revealed herself during the difficult lockdown we all had to live through.

Venetians have been blessed: all of a sudden Venice was empty. No more restaurants nor cafes nor shopping. No people around ....

Two months of glorious, shining days, sky like a pure crystal, and nobody there.

Just us last Venetians left, trying to escape controls just to take a promenade and find the real Venice.

Blessed—no other word could be enough to express the perfect beauty we were looking at: beautiful monuments, precious marbles, white, red or blue or green, elegant *triforas*—those most iconic of Venetian windows—and ... silence.

No motorboats nor taxis nor gondolas. The city seemed to be within a dream. Venice seemed to be finally breathing and opening her arms to embrace the Lagoon that was so quiet: not even one boat ... and the water so clean, so transparent .... The sky and architecture reflecting in the water seemed to be a *miraggio*. Was it real? Was it a dream?

A gift, I would say, a priceless gift for us, revealing the sense of silence, the need to let the pure beauty enter inside myself and fulfil my heart. The Lagoon itself seemed like it was enjoying this new dimension.

Will this dream last? How long?

We have to think about a new kind of tourism, a respectful one, a conscious one, that kind of tourist who feels what it's like being in a place nobody can repeat, a tourist who knows that only silence, respectful silence, is the right attitude.

Biography

Francesca Barozzi is descended from one of the oldest and noblest Venetian families, listed in the Libro d'Oro. *She studied ancient Christian archaeology in the University of Padua. Her husband's family is connected to the Vidal cosmetic business where Francesca works in business management and administration. She is also Vice President of the Venetian Soroptimist Club and Vice Delegate of Venetian Accademia Italiana della Cucina.*

**"Venice, Piazza San Marco, April 2020,
Covid-19 Time, 02:00 a.m."
by Piero Bellini**

... I can hear the echo of my steps ...

Biography

Piero Bellini, born in 1958 in Venice, still lives in the city with his wife Lorenza and their son Oscar. He works for a local bank and for many years was a dealer in the foreign exchange and money market. Piero is the author of the humorous book MATTAMATICA (Madmath) and also a book about British war economy and finance during World War II. Piero's hobby is jazz music, and he plays piano and composes together with other Venetian friends. Hear his music, with images of Venice during the pandemic, at https://youtu.be/rMr3_ElnqyE

"Venice, Queen of Strength and Beauty"
by Mariangela Bognolo

Venice!

You have bewitched my heart ... my enchanted soul!

Just saying her name makes your heart beat and pervade your soul. City of pure poetry where beauty is not only an aesthetic concept but pure reality.

Those who arrive in this city are catapulted into a dream. It "excites all that is poetic in us, unleashes our faculties of admiration," and with these words Guy de Maupassant perfectly describes Venice's appearance and his deep feelings.

Lots of artists, writers, musicians, and collectors have walked through the streets and lived here: Dante, Canaletto, Tiziano, Tintoretto, Lord Byron, Goethe, Hemingway, Wagner, Peggy Guggenheim ... just to name a few without counting all those personalities to whom Venice gave birth.

In short, Venice is not only the city of tourists; it is much more—it is a lifestyle!

It is a city that hides wonders and an illustrious past—a past that you can still breathe in the air, you can smell the wood mixed with the salt inside the ancient buildings, you can feel it walking through the streets when you detect a sweet scent of pancakes, you can smell old library books. We can still perceive that atmosphere that dates back to ancient Venice when it was a maritime power.

Despite remembering the glorious past, Venice never stops. Carnevale, Biennale, Film Festival, contemporary art exhibitions ... it is a city in perpetual movement, day and night.

Taxis, boats, and *vaporetti* run up and down the Grand Canal and the Lagoon. People chat from one window to another, we say goodbye from one boat to another ... here everything is joy!

It is wonderful to get lost in the *calli* admiring the houses that make us think of "natural places," as Marcel Proust defined them, places of great and respectable human strength, Goethe would say instead.

Despite all this, there is no frenzy in Venice. It seems a contradiction, but it is pure truth. It is like looking at a work of art, having time and getting lost in it. The mind wanders far away, and nothing matters anymore.

Venice is a stage, an open-air theater full of twists and turns that leaves you breathless until the end.

High water is also one of the characteristics of this city. In autumn, depending on the tides, the waters of the Lagoon slowly invade the foundations, arrive in Piazza San Marco, and life goes on normally as always. The Lagoon, however, sometimes takes over, and in a moment the scenario changes as it happened in November 2019.

A strong wind and torrential rain hit the city, creating an almost apocalyptic scenario. The wind hissed and did not stop, its fury dragging the water over the banks and bringing more and more to overwhelm the whole city. People were locked up in their homes, and everyone's mind was experiencing the tremendous flood of 1966. By just a few centimeters, the water did not reach this height, but the fear and the damage were great. For a moment Venice was brought to its knees, but soon, thanks to the strength of its inhabitants, it returned to its previous splendor.

Christmas, New Year's Eve, and Carnevale followed soon after. The latter is the most beautiful, festive, and colorful moment. The city is filled with sumptuous costumes and masked faces. Everything takes on a different atmosphere, and in an instant you are catapulted into a painting by Canaletto or Pietro Longhi. Suddenly, however, a mysterious shadow enveloped the whole world and even Venice itself ... the fear of a Covid-19 epidemic.

The big Carnevale machine stopped. Everything was canceled. People began to lock themselves in the house again, eagerly waiting for the end of that nightmare.

Venice became a ghost town. No one on the *calli* and *fondamente*, no boats in the Lagoon. The shops, museums, and churches were closed, and the only sounds that could be heard were the gurgling of the water, the sound of seagulls, and the bells that kept ringing the hours.

The darkness greatly enhanced this aspect of loneliness and melancholy, but on beautiful, sunny days people noticed how the waters of the Lagoon were tinged with emerald green never seen before. Marine fauna, for the first time, entered the city, and at that moment it became clear how nature took over the world and locked man in a cage. The silent architecture of the Grand Canal was reflected in those emerald waters "like a mirror to which they rely without fear. A mirror that can hide the ugly truth of wrinkles by highlighting the secret of the most seductive makeup"; these words of Mieczysław Kozłowski contain a great truth, the Venetian reality.

Slowly life began to flow even slower. The city came back to life but not as before. Today there is still fear and this is a deep wound for Venice, but she will soon rise again as the phoenix rises from her ashes and will still be more beautiful and wonderful. It doesn't matter if architecturally or environmentally nothing has changed, but we have changed our thoughts and emotions.

We will know how to love and respect Venice even more because she is the Queen just as Paolo Veronese painted her, and her beauty and strength will continue for many centuries.

Biography

Mariangela Bognolo, born in 1982, is a critic and art historian. She has written several articles on art history and lectured for FAI. She has been present in the juries of various competitions and presented exhibitions in different Italian cities. On January 5, 2019, she was awarded the Voltaire prize for criticism. She collaborates with the architect Maurizio Galeone on the subject of the Progenitor Art. Mariangela is a radio speaker, head of the Cultural Heritage department of CAD Venice, member of the "Il Castello" Association, ambassador of culture for Spirito Nuovo Venice, and part of the Soroptimist Club Miranese - Riviera del Brenta.

"L'Arazzo Vivente"
di Manuela Brunello

Vivo a Venezia per una scelta, elaborata 8 anni fa da un'occasione favorevole creatasi e presa al volo, e affrontata come atto di coraggio, perché cambiare consuetudini per lanciarsi nell'incognita di una città così ricca di contrasti ha richiesto appunto coraggio. Da Mestre, dove abitavo, l'ho sempre vissuta come una presenza straordinaria, potendola osservare dalla terraferma come uno scrigno ricco di tesori, ma non per questo facile soprattutto ai giorni nostri, perché vivendo fra questi tesori, se non la si vive con rispetto e molta umiltà si può restare pericolosamente incagliati.

Una cosa è fondamentale: la consapevolezza che per tutto quello che da, dovrà esserci da parte di ognuno una restituzione. Accettando e vivendo come privilegio un ritmo di vita oggi unico e irripetibile. Essere immersi nella bellezza, che a Venezia non è ferma alla staticità dei meravigliosi monumenti, fa sì che si possa vivere in diretta e mettere in scena un'esistenza più consona all'essere umano, vivere una città nel terzo millennio assaporandone le tradizioni rimaste vive e che restituiscono un quotidiano che altrove è sparito. Una rete di piccole cose, tra canali e calli, che fa di questa città un merletto vivente, ha impedito l'invasione di tante modernità, preservandola e conservandola.

Ogni giorno Venezia combatte una guerra contro un'invasione barbarica di "entità" che la vogliono fare loro, come un bottino di guerra, attingendo a piene mani e depredandola. Ma Venezia è Venezia, nata per sfuggire alle invasioni, che nei suoi secoli ha sempre dovuto combattere, e ne è abituata, è di spirito, scaltra, intelligente ironica e poco incline a essere sopraffatta. Vende cara la sua pelle, così non fosse di lei avremmo, ai nostri giorni, un lontano e vago ricordo.

Il problema è che l'umanità impara dagli errori che commette, e spesso diventa molto tardi per avvenersene. Una città vive e palpita in connessione con i suoi abitanti, che abitandola costruiscono ogni giorno, in base alle necessità, un flusso di impercettibili o grandi mutamenti che sono il materiale per fare sì che si trasformi continuamente in modo vantaggioso per una conservazione della vita. Un tempo tutto passava attraverso un'umanità la cui forte consapevolezza dava la possibilità di esercitare una sorta di saggezza. Fino a un centinaio di anni fa era tutto creato con le mani, e questo faceva sì che ogni azione passasse attraverso il filtro dell'esperienza, e ogni manifattura fosse il risultato di un lavoro che intrecciava corpo e anima.

Oggi, con il web siamo arrivati in poco tempo a un estraniamento così radicale, e ci siamo spostati in un ambito che lascia da parte il corpo / anima e rende protagonista una virtualità che non può essere in grado di generare tutte le risposte alle necessità giornaliere. Così assistiamo alla nascita di progetti totalmente avulsi e lontani da noi, con l'illusione che siano risolutivi, impiegando energie enormi che resteranno in eredità come scheletri inutilizzabili e ingombranti.

A Venezia l'acqua alta è il risultato di anni di inesperienze accumulate, di progettualità sbagliate, e ciò che è capitato quest'anno purtroppo credo sia solo l'inizio di un tempo in cui l'eccezionalità non sarà più eccezionale, ma usuale. Quest'anno l'acqua alta di novembre si era già annunciata l'anno scorso, dove lo studio in cui lavoro, dipingo, si era allagato in modo meno invasivo, ma con una promessa, "ci vediamo il prossimo anno," regolarmente mantenuta. E l'acqua è arrivata, inesorabile, invadendo un luogo che mai era stato allagato così gravemente. Certamente c'era stato il tempo per me di alzare i pochi mobili, i quadri, i tappeti. Lavoro che se anche minimo richiede un forte dispendio di energie, e quando succede, il giorno dopo si contano i morti. Questa batosta per la città ha fatto sì che l'afflusso del turismo cominciasse ad avere un primo arresto importante.

Dove lavoro, zona ricca di gallerie d'arte e di antiquariato, e negozi di qualità, è una nicchia poco conosciuta e di passaggio molto rado. Essere artisti è comunque difficile perché offri un lavoro spesso considerato non necessario, soprattutto in alcuni periodi. La nostra zona, così ricca di arte manifatturiera vive molto del passaggio che si crea con le persone che vanno a visitare le mostre di Palazzo Grassi. Allora, rialzatici in piedi dopo l'acqua di novembre, tutta la speranza di una ripartenza era anche focalizzata su una mostra importante in apertura a marzo, che avrebbe sicuramente creato un importante movimento di viaggiatori realmente interessati all'arte. E quindi, pensiamo positivo, cercando di tenere duro, andiamo avanti.... Neanche il tempo per ristabilizzarsi e appare una nuova minaccia, invisibile ed estremamente invasiva, la pandemia, tutti confinati nelle case. I giorni precedenti a questa chiusura totale avevano già mostrato una Venezia deserta: immagini incredibili, per il passaggio repentino da una situazione ormai fuori controllo di un turismo vampiro, arrogante di folle di predatori di visioni ed energie, ormai fuori controllo a quella del deserto totale, all'improvviso non c'era più nessuno... Mi sono chiesta allora, ma nel mezzo cosa ci sta?

Quando ho capito cosa realmente ci aspettava, ho preso un carretto di materiale per lavorare e come tutti ho sperimentato una nuova vita, #iorestoacasa, il confronto giornaliero con difficoltà da affrontare, ma utile per riflettere e capire che basta un attimo, e si può e si deve vivere con rispetto, se non vogliamo che la situazione precipiti. Rispetto è la rinuncia al dovere fare prevalere il nostro ego e la capacità di mettersi nei panni dell'altro, arrivando in sostanza a "non fare agli altri ciò che non vorresti fosse fatto a te." So che poi, quando passano i problemi, la tendenza è tornare come prima, ma la notizia è che per un po' così non potrà essere, e viaggiando in questo limbo straordinario, si possono elaborare molte soluzioni che abbiano il rispetto come denominatore. È necessario. E potrà essere un cambiamento vantaggioso per tutti.

Sono tornata a dipingere da alcuni giorni al mio studio, la fase di un ritorno alla normalità sarà lunga, nel mio piccolo amo creare situazioni che per me sono di bellezza e armonia, e se il messaggio viene recepito, so che per un momento, pari ad una goccia in un oceano, potrò regalare un istante di miglioramento, perchè la bellezza migliora. E questo è il contributo che voglio portare a Venezia, e per questo mi impegno e cercherò di resistere.

Biografia

Vivo e lavoro a Venezia, dove ho uno studio nei pressi di Palazzo Grassi. Sulle orme della tradizione veneziana, la mia opera nasce dalla ricerca e l'interpretazione di forme, strutture e superfici di oggetti, che vengono rappresentati attraverso l'attenzione assoluta del ritratto, dove l'oggetto è riletto con una tecnica che usa l'intreccio accompagnato ad una tridimensionalità, e "fermato" in una situazione di rappresentazione iconica. Questa serie di oggetti durante il percorso, si è arricchita di "temi," e i ritratti dipinti rappresentano animali, vestiti e oggetti. Ho partecipato a varie mostre sia personali che collettive, dipingo da circa 10 anni dopo un periodo in cui realizzavo gioielli in perle di vetro, e due anni di frequentazione dell'Accademia di Belle Arti di Venezia.

"A Long Life to Venice!"
by Vera Brunello

I'm a lucky woman for more than one reason.

One reason is that I live in Jesolo, a seaside resort 50 kilometers from Venice. I can reach it by car or by boat. When I was a child, my parents loved to enjoy art, so I remember many trips to Venice, visiting the Biennale, Palazzo Ducale, the Torre dell'Orologio, and many exhibitions and beautiful places. I loved very much the trip by boat, especially in the evening, coming back to Jesolo: the lights far away in the dark, the sound of the *motonave* sliding on the water, the stars and the moon.

When I was fourteen, I began high school in Venice at the Institute for Tourism "Algarotti," which is located at Ca' Savorgnan, a palace on the Rio Cannaregio. I was in love with that school, and I felt proud and privileged to be a student in Venice. Even though I went there every day and the journey lasted an hour on the way and an hour on the way back, I always looked at my school with wonder.

However, studying in Venice had some strange aspects; for example, hours of physical education often took place in deconsecrated churches or convents. So my classmates and I ran in a row among ancient columns, and the sound of our footsteps echoed in that space laden with history.

One day at school the water level started to rise quickly in the mid-morning, and the school closed to allow students to return home. But water was already everywhere, and my friend and I didn't know how to cross a part of Lista di Spagna to reach the *vaporetto* stop at Ponte degli Scalzi and get to Piazzale Roma with our shoes still dry. Our Venetian math teacher, who came from home with his high rubber boots, offered to help. We ended up crossing the water in our professor's arms.

Twenty years later, my daughter began studying at the same school. I was a little worried: I wondered how much my enthusiastic stories had influenced her choice.

Maybe she had a too romantic idea about that school.

But when we entered Ca' Savorgnan for the orientation visit, I saw a light in her eyes; and when they led us to the *Aula Magna* that was in the restored chapel of the palace, she opened her eyes wide and said, "Mum, this is my school!" The chapel, which in my time was closed and hidden, was marvelous: high white and golden ceilings, statues, stuccos—magnificence.

But what else can we expect in Venice?

So, it was a pleasure to study in those magical rooms, in the colors of a completely frescoed library, and to walk on floors made of Venetian *terrazzo*. Looking out of the large windows, you could see moments of real Venetian life.

Once, I went to a parent-teacher conference, taking my eight-year-old son with me. We arrived too early and had to wait in the salon on the first floor, sitting on a beautiful blue and golden Venetian-style sofa. He looked around and said, "Mum, I want to go to such a beautiful school too! With this beautiful sofa!"

And many years later, he studied and graduated at IED, the European Institute for Design, at Palazzo Cavalli-Franchetti, next to the Accademia Bridge and overlooking the Grand Canal. Grand staircases, high mullioned windows, and an amazing *Aula Magna*: with a wooden neogothic-style bookcase and shelving, with two little spiral stairs leading to the upper part of the shelves. Dark wood everywhere, and that marvelous view, whether you look out onto the Grand Canal or you look out onto the garden.

Well, Venice is not just beauty and poetry and art—it is also a place where young minds are fed and cultivated, and relationships and friendships are born, and all these young people roam around Venice and make it sparkling and lively.

But now we are living in very strange times. Covid-19 has forced us to stop our normal lives, and we are seeing a world that we had only seen in science fiction movies.

So, my beautiful Venice is now empty and silenced. No more tourists, no more students, no more Venetians. No more a mix of languages, no more workers shouting *"Ocio ae gambe!"* ("Watch your legs!" which is the way the transporters of goods by hand trolleys warn the people to move in the narrow Venetian *calli*).

No more voices and laughter. No more gondolas with a singing gondolier in the narrow, romantic canals. No more gondoliers on the little bridges with their striped shirts and straw hats saying, "Gondola, *signori*, gondola!"

I see a deserted city, and I imagine the empty museums and palaces: all those wonderful paintings and sculptures, now in the dark, waiting for somebody to look at them again with emotion and amazement.

But the city is now breathing. The water in the canals is clear and full of life: someone has seen a jellyfish, a seahorse, but more simply, a lot of fish and some ducks, and in the silence, their squawking brings joy.

It's a good thing that there are no more cruise ships passing through the Giudecca Canal and the San Marco basin like scary giants; and all those tourists, too many, all together, mistreat the ancient streets dragging their luggage. You can't deeply enjoy the beauty of Venice if you are always surrounded by thousands of people.

This is not anger against tourists, because they are necessary for the city to live and survive, and also Venice is a jewel that must be admired, and the wonder that it arouses in people is part of its life. But another way must be found.

As for me, I spent the lockdown period with my children and my sister who lives below us. It was frightening to hear the terrible news and see the situation in Bergamo on TV: in the silence of the deserted streets, only the deafening and continuous sound of the ambulances running, day and night, to bring to the hospital people who couldn't breathe. And all this horror, among the pink trees in bloom, with spring exploding.

I felt safe at home, and I only went out to the supermarket. The weather was beautiful and sunny, and we spent our afternoons on the terrace, sunbathing, reading, talking, and petting our two cats. There was an incredible silence, broken only by the voices of different birds. There was a sort of magic in that situation, and looking at the birds, I wondered how they were feeling without humans around and without the noise and pollution we cause.

It's true that it was like humans were in cages and animals were free. A bad moment for people but a beautiful and peaceful moment for nature.

I returned to Venice on May 20. From the 18th, you could leave your town, but there were very few people around. Venice was there, in all its majesty, in a dress never worn before. It was incredible to cross the empty Ponte dei Sospiri. Everything around us seemed lighter: the white of marble seemed whiter, and my friend and I saw the Palazzo Ducale in a way we had never seen it before, because of the wall of people always standing at that point of the *fondamenta*. We laughed happily and went on saying, "*Che meraviglia*!"

And all those parked gondolas, dancing on the little waves of the San Marco basin! The view of San Giorgio Island, in front of Piazza San Marco, had never been so clear when there was normal boat traffic.

There was an unreal atmosphere. The silence, first of all, and the long views, as far as the eye can go. Although this situation came from a terrible thing, it was a gift to enjoy my beloved Venice in this unimaginable and, I think, unrepeatable way. This experience made me reflect once again on how necessary it is to regulate the flow of visitors.

And it's time to protect Venice from high water, seriously and quickly. Now.

The whole world saw the images of the frightening night of last November. Living 300 meters from the beach, I heard the fury of the wind and the scream of the sea, and I saw on Facebook what was happening to some of my Venetian friends.

One of them wrote, "I recently came home, thanks to a friend who literally saved me, defying this terrible weather to take me to the Island of Giudecca. I walked in the dark, with the water that reached my belly, while cold waves slammed against the *fondamenta* and reached the walls, even breaking through the doors. The icy splashes came over my head, the *scirocco* wind blew at 100 km/h, I had to be dodging the *passarelle* walkways in the high water carried by the waves."

On the way, she found a little sheltered place and filmed the situation for a few minutes. Really scary!

That night, around midnight, the wind stopped. My daughter and I decided to go out by car to see what had just happened. The sea had reached the main street, 200 meters beyond the shore. On the asphalt remained a dense foam, sand, and pieces of wood. Everywhere, overturned garbage cans, some broken branches, and a carpet of pine needles.

The day after, we went out for a walk, and we saw one thing that gave us an idea of how powerful the force of the sea had been. On a little road that leads to the beach, about five meters wide and leading to a tall hotel, we saw signs of foam and sand up to the third floor. It's very high, and it was scary to imagine the situation. And it was easy to understand why Venice had been devastated.

But even "normal" high water is a big problem, although this strange phenomenon is definitely distinctive and even fascinating for tourists. Unfortunately, water ruins the artistic heritage of Venice and makes life very difficult for those who live and work in the city.

But the solution is a real puzzle.

Every now and then, some scholar comes up with a new way to save Venice from the *acqua alta*, but I think that, unfortunately, the validity of a method can be proven just by applying it in reality, like with the MOSE Project. For a long time we thought and hoped that it was the answer, but it seems it is not.

I think that it's impossible to predict all the facets, eventualities, and consequences that could happen. For this reason, perhaps we should start with the simplest things, like digging the bottom of the canals, which over the centuries have filled up a lot.

Venice must be treated with great care and delicacy.

Big ships must no longer endanger the city.

Tourists must arrive with reservations, so there are not too many of them all together, but all must be able to enjoy the magic of the city.

Because Venice lives in its history and art and beauty, but also in the memories and the stories of all those who love it.

A long life to Venice!

Biography

Vera Brunello was born in 1965 and lives in Jesolo with her two children. Her passion is sports: she taught artistic gymnastics for 15 years, and now she teaches volleyball to children of five, six, and seven years. She attended "Algarotti" high school in Venice for five years, and in this period she collected many fun and special experiences. She has always continued to love Venice and does not miss an opportunity to enjoy its events, discover new places, and meet new friends from all over the world.

"A Catalyst"
by Manuel Carrión with Kathleen González

On May 17, 2020, I talked with artist Manuel Carrión while he was strolling in the Biennale Gardini and I was at home in California. Our 45-minute conversation ranged over many topics. The following excerpt has been edited for brevity and clarity to capture Manuel's thoughts during the time of Covid-19. My comments are in italics. KG

"These days I'm literally learning the secrets of nature, that are hidden in front of us. We don't have to search a lot. They are here. We have to open our minds, our souls, our spirits, our bodies, to listen."

"Yes, I think there's so much there if we stop, take the time, and tune into those messages that are there."

"Yeah, yeah."

"You know, the school I teach at is run by Benedictine monks."

"Beautiful."

"The Benedictine monks have this idea of listening 'with the ear of the heart.' Opening your heart to people and listening to what they say, with your heart and not just your ears. I think it's really a nice idea."

"This message is very helpful for me in this moment. My heart is … is going too fast because I am in love with everything. Man woman trees nature sand cats beaches everything. Even the emotions that sometimes make us angry—I think even those emotions are something that we must love and learn from them."

"Yes, I think that's true. So how does this relate for you to the time that Venice is going through?"

"Well, as I told you the other day, the 22nd of March, they announced this lockdown, and myself, I have been in a process of evolution. From the 16th of March to the first of June, that means 108 days, I started this process. I don't know what it is in English. I have transformed in a *catalizzatore*."

"I'm opening up the translator on my computer to look it up. Catalizzatore. *Oh, okay, a catalyst."*

"Yeah. So I have been transformed in a catalyst for 108 days, both the positive and negative energy. So in this moment I feel like a very powerful entity."

"Oh, wow. How do you determine this?"

"Because we have to have faith. You have to have faith in something, then things come true. The power of our mind is very, very big. When we are living in this moment, it's just the process of something that we are building in our minds. So the person that knows about it, they must work in the light and in the shadow."

"Like the yin and yang, the way the two play with each other."

"You have to do it sharing your knowledge, but you have to do it not getting some credit for it. It's one of the most important rules."

"So with a lot of humility."

"You do something as Benedictines, you just have to listen with your heart, you must do it with your soul, without anything in exchange. Each time you receive a new method, each time you receive new knowledge, each time you receive a new emotion, a feeling, you have to return it. Little things, maybe, with a flower, with a kiss, with a smile, and share with the world around yourself and not just that, with another entity."

"I think that's so important right now when so many people are hurting, or are afraid or are lonely. Any of us, even if we're healthy or if we have troubles, we have to try to remember to spread that positive energy and not just dwell on the negative parts. Because when we dwell on the negative parts, we continue to manifest more of the negative."

"And, Kathy, for me it's been very hard because I have met other people who have had this knowledge for a long time, and I just now understand this process, this coronavirus, and I think I'm very grateful to Venice for it because in this moment of our history, Venice is the most peaceful place in the world, at least for me, to be. I don't know for other people. Each person has to create their own reality, and has to choose where to stay and not to stay. I take the position to stay in Venice and it is very, very nice.

"Venice has a mix of all the cultures. People come here from all over the world, and we share everything, so we have the attributes of all humanity. That's one of my philosophies. And the second of my philosophies is that in Venice there is too much beauty. There is the light. There is the water. People can be happy even in the moment of shadow. Happiness, I think, is our tool for surviving, if we decide to survive."

"Right. You know, I've been lucky enough to study some things about the neuroscience of learning and how our brains work, and when we have fear, or we don't feel safe, it closes the amygdala, which is the 'gate' in the middle of the brain that allows information to pass through. And so if you have an 'amygdala hijack,' like a hijacker on an airplane, that fear will shut down your brain so that you can't learn, or you can't access the information that you have."

"Most of humanity, for a period of time, were very stressed. So if people are afraid of Manuel Carrión, I am going to be afraid also.

"In this moment, 2020, Venice is loved. But I received so much fear from all those other people, and that energy arrived directly to my heart. I have a very connected heart with the people around myself. As I told you the other day, I built a rainbow. It was in many places: in Venice, in Gorizia, in San Doná, London, Quito, just with my mind."

"Hmm hmm."

"I think what is happening now, is people are returning to themselves, to be part of this universe and to build something that is bigger than we are. But this process is just nature, it is nothing new."

"So you were telling me the other day about what happened on Giudecca, about how the people became closer to their neighbors and the community."

"What I understand is that each community, each place, has their own reality. They have other ways of sharing things, of communicating things. Even my neighbors—I have three houses next to me, the one of Francesca, which has six people, another one with three, and me, I was alone. But it's important to comprehend that Giudecca where I live was very peaceful, because there has been sunshine, we have gardens, we have community, we decide our own rules.

"So we have to rebuild a new society in which each city has its own body and we have to put in the mind, the heart, the soul, and the spirit. Some are going to be more commercial, some are going to be more emotional, some are going to be more for living. But what is happening now is that cities are in chaos. When I go to New York, when I go to London, when I go to Mestre, when I go to Padova, I don't understand any more. There is no more order, just a lot of chaos. There is not an organization inside the community in order to create equilibrium. And this is very important to understand because this is going to be the future—that communities must live with order in small territories and population. As has happened in Venice now. So what could happen is in big cities, with more than millions of people, we have to divide those cities and reorganize and understand which part is the body, which part is the hand, which part is the heart. We have to return to the medieval. In the medieval period, in the cities, the gardens were organized in the way that everything was very natural."

"But the medieval times were considered a time of darkness, when there was a lot of fear and ignorance. How do we transform it into something positive?"

"Well, I think the medieval was the period in which kings, queens, princes, princesses, established the rules of our society. But the origin of all these things was with Dante. He said that *il uomo nobile* (and Carrión would say that *il uomo e la donna nobili*) will be able to educate others to be noble with nature, with the society, with themselves. When they want too much power, too much money, and they won't share it, when the kings, the queens, the princes, the princesses have too much power, they have too many titles, and they didn't share it. And in a way there was darkness in their society. Like now, we are in a dark cycle for our society in our economy."

"Uh huh."

"The economy right now is in total disequilibrium with the political part, with the spiritual part, with the creative part. We have to return to a way in which the politics, the economy, the arts and the culture, the roots of our society return to an equilibrium with itself. Otherwise, we'll disconnect as we are doing now. In the first medieval period, there was equilibrium. That was the period of Dante, and also the period of San Francesco. And I think we have a lot of messages from that period. Now we are repeating life after the medieval period. In this moment of our society, just two percent of the population has all the money, has all the power, in the whole world."

"Hmm hmm."

"That's totally in disequilibrium. It's not right, this thing. It's not possible. People delegate power to politicians and to the rules of others. And that is not fair. Because we are the polity. I think people have to return to decide in a 50/50 way."

"Yes, going back to that classic period of ancient Greece."

"Yes, a classic, but also a futuristic. We always need to have a foot in the past and a foot in the future. But we must live in the present time without forgetting about our past or our future. But now we are living neither in the past, neither in the present, neither in the future. We are living in an illusion of others. We must accept our nature and be ourselves.

"I'm going to go to San Marco now and will send you some pictures, Kathy. It's magic. It's magic magic magic. It's incredible to see all these people happy, returning to life, to normality. It's just the most beautiful thing that has happened in all this *pandemia*. And I'm very happy that things are going in the right way."

"I love the picture that you sent of the sun going down over the water. Everything is silver."

"Okay, Kathy, now I'm with Natasha and Giuseppe, I'm going to take a spritz with them. And whenever you want we can have more dialogues for the book. I'm very happy, very blessed. I want to study more about the Benedictines. It's important for me to understand these different cultures."

"Yes, Saint Benedict was really a wise man. I think that the things he taught are a wonderful way to live with others. Alright,

Manuel, it was really nice to talk with you. Enjoy your spritz. Enjoy the Piazza."

"Big big hug and kisses. Take care."

Biography

Manuel Carrión is an Ecuadorian artist, born in Quito on September 23rd, 1983. With intense effort, he has produced countless works, which can be found around the world, mainly in Venice, Paris, New York, Kyoto, and Quito. The aqua granda *and a subsequent fire destroyed his gallery on Giudecca and much of his artwork. Visit manuelcarrion.com*

"Venetian Soul"
by Monica Cesarato

"I have had dreams and I have had nightmares, but I have conquered my nightmares because of my dreams."
--Jonas Salk

As you all know, the nightmare in Venice started in November 2019, not in 2020. The *aqua granda* caught everyone by surprise and, even though people were back on their feet cleaning and bleaching the very next morning, no one would have imagined that the terrible month of November would be the preamble of a much more serious epoch.

By the beginning of December, it was already pretty clear tourists were not coming back yet to the city: bombarded by the media with dramatic images and videos of the night between November 12th and 13th and its aftermath, misinformed by the real situation in the city by foreign journalists who did not really care about the damage they were causing to the city's image, many people who had booked their December holidays were fast canceling reservations all over the city.

Talk all over town was about how sad and worrying this was.

But we had high hopes for Carnevale. Yes, come on, Carnevale is always packed with crowds in Venice. Surely people will come back to our city to enjoy one of the most incredible times of the year!

But, truth be told, even during Carnevale, we realized something was not right: hotels were not fully booked, the streets were not packed with crowds, Piazza San Marco was not as full as always!

We blamed it on the bad publicity, on the fact that it was February and cold, etc. etc. We told ourselves: things will get better with Spring, you will see!

And then disaster: the best and last days of Carnevale got canceled for safety reasons—and rightly so! I'm not debating that.

And we still told ourselves: it is only for a few days, then they will all come back, you'll see. People love Venice! We will be okay.

Or so we thought!

Enter Covid-19. Enter lockdown and with it an even worse nightmare, with no end yet.

Condensed in a few sentences, this is what has been happening in Venice in the last nine months!

And how did I feel about it?

I am overall a very positive person, trying always to make do with what I have. And throughout these months, I made a precise point, all during lockdown, to only post positive thoughts on social media; to try to connect with people even more than I usually do, above all if I knew they were living alone and quarantined; to try to not let the darkness engulf me.

It has not been easy, much more so with no income coming through, a family to support by myself, surrounded by people in the same exact situation.

When I thought of putting down my emotions and feelings about these terrible times for a chapter in a book, I agreed immediately, but then I started to postpone and postpone—a strange apathy embraced me. Not because I did not have anything to say, but simply I felt that if I stopped and actually wrote how I really felt, maybe this would be the time I finally broke down, after having managed to hang in there and stay positive for so long.

Yet my positive attitude has prevailed again: I am not going to talk to you about the nightmares of the lockdown; of the sense of despair we all have been going through; of the fact that we will not probably see tourists coming back to Venice till maybe 2021 with the consequences of a huge economical disaster; of the fact that we are all financially broke and wondering when all of this will end.

We are all in the same boat: everybody has a bad story to tell and to shed tears about—no need to add mine, too.

No, I am going to talk to you about a dream. A dream to help Venice, which I had during the lockdown. A dream that I will try, with all my strength, to turn into a reality. A dream that I hope all the lovers of Venice will help achieve.

Because nightmares can be turned into sweet dreams, as long as you do your best to change the endings. Simple as that!

So here is the story of a dream called *Anima Veneziana*!

Three a.m., May 10th, 2020: I suddenly woke up all excited. I had the most amazing dream! Actually, it was more than a dream: it was an idea!

Too bad I had to wait till morning to share it with my friends to see if it was, in fact, a good idea or, rather, some crazy unfeasible dream, born out of frustration from the lockdown.

So, early on a Sunday morning, I called Romena Brugnerotto, of RomInVenice, a local tour guide and travel blogger—my partner in crime for many Venetian adventures!

The night before we had discussed live on Instagram with our followers the fact that we were pretty fed up with seeing all those videos of an empty Venice during lockdown, all showing the "usual" iconic monuments, kind of declaring the death of the city and its citizens.

No, Venice was not dead! This needed to be told!

And that was what my dream was all about: a film showing the world a "Living Venice," with its inhabitants and those working there, in normal, daily life!

I dreamt that Venice itself was telling the story.

I explained to Romena my dream; I told her the story (which is still top secret of course—you will have to wait to see the film for that), and after a moment of silence, she kind of gave out a little sob. Surprised, I asked her what was happening, and she replied, "You just made me cry. It's beautiful!"

I called some other friends, and the reaction was practically the same.

"Mmmm, okay, this might just be a good idea, after all," I thought.

I am a dreamer, I know, but I am also a very practical and go-and-do person, as those who really know me are aware of. I have big crazy dreams, but I also know that they need to be practical, not just pretty!

I immediately got in contact with a Venetian film director in Los Angeles and explained my plan. I was expecting him to just laugh out loud. Instead he told me he loved the idea, and it could be done.

He put me in touch with Federico Bizzarini, renowned Venetian film director, who I accidentally worked with during the last Venice Carnevale, for a cooking class with the Festa delle Marie. Federico's first reaction was a good long silence, then he immediately started to tell me what and how to do the film and who to involve. "Okay," I thought, "he likes it too."

Federico then spoke to Lorenzo Pezzano, famous director of photography, with a long career in filming in Venice. Lorenzo, after a long silence (yes, everybody was a bit shocked at first) told me it could be done, but since we were not talking about a mom-and-pop video, but something seriously professional, the budget could not be low.

I grinned, because all I was hearing was: "It can be done!"

Skip to July 2020, literally two months later: *Anima Veneziana's* crowd funding has been launched!

The business plan is done, we gathered the support of so many local Venetian associations, businesses, and residents, and we have the support of a reliable, established nonprofit association! Looks like we are set!

Oh no, wait: we need money, lots of money, tons of money! Fifty thousand euros! Hence the crowdfunding!

Anima Veneziana is a gift to the city of Venice, made by those who love her dearly.

Anima Veneziana is a project involving a brighter side of Venice and the Venetians. It is nonpartisan and nonprofit. The involvement of all those who are taking part in it has been broad and sincere right from the start: hearts that beat to the rhythm of the same love.

Anima Veneziana is a short film that tells about Venice as the Venetians live and know it: a city worth visiting for more than two days, an ideal place that is the fruit of centuries of history and love. It was born from the desire to change the narrative of the city, plagued by the stories of her umpteenth death after high water and the closure during Covid-19. Despite evident difficulties, her citizens have never given up and have, indeed, found new energy and are now ready to face new challenges.

Anima Veneziana is the story of a bright, pulsating, and vibrant city, made by real people who offer their arts, their talent, and their passion as an antidote to the death that many are always ready to announce. Not a city seen by drones, and not only iconic places. A city inhabited by Venetians, famous for their vision and their stubbornness: not actors, therefore, but citizens in flesh and blood, gathered around Venetian art and craftsmanship. The film will highlight the various aspects of life in Venice: the moments of the day, the various categories of those who live and those who work there every day.

It is not a film about the iconic monuments of Venice but a documentary about Venice as a whole, intended as a city with all its inhabitants. It stems from the desire to make the real Venice known to the world, a Venice that must be discovered in depth, something that cannot be done in a couple of days' visit.

Making this short film means promoting the city and, once made, it will be available to all those who want to use it.

There!

You all probably think I am crazy to embark on something like this, right now with no work and a difficult financial situation.

But it turns out there are a lot of crazy Venetians around, because when I started to explain what I was planning to do, so many residents and businesses, even though they are on their knees struggling after the *aqua granda*, the lockdown, and the lack of work, have given me their total support, either offering their location for filming or offering their products and services for the crowdfunding.

And it turns out this project is doing something that has never been done before. It is bringing Venetians together, all working with one mission: to show the world that there is an authentic Venice still waiting to be discovered.

To all of those out there who truly love Venice: you have a new film to look forward to!

Biography

Monica Cesarato, food and travel blogger, Venice lover, cooking instructor, and food guide, but simply an overall talker—creator of #aphotoofveniceaday
Twitter: @monicacesarato.com @cookinvenice
Facebook: Monica Cesarato and Cook In Venice
Instagram: @monicacesarato, @cookinvenice @aphotoofveniceaday
Www.animaveneziana.com

"The Tank"
by Caterina Codato

There are nebulous days that appear slowed down right from the first light of dawn, like a woman struggling to carry her burden along the steep path that life has for her. Days like this take your breath away, drowning it in damp rales, while waiting for the coolness of the storm, and the sea refuses to drive away the tide that inexorably, silently, rises ... rises ... rises ....

These are the days of *acqua alta*, the high tide, of the fatigue of the residents, but also of the gangways along the *calli*, of the joyful tourists with their cameras and selfies, these are the days of a Piazza San Marco that looks like a princess' mirror, where the sky is painted with colors above the ancient cobblestones, asking the city who could ever be the fairest of them all.

The water slowly rises and leaves time for the city to get ready, to put on the boots, to raise the bulkheads and store belongings in many small tanks, each with its own secrets.

Even on that foggy November evening, the city seemed to be about to face one of these days but, as the day was drawing to a close, strangely enough, the sky became more and more sinister, darker, of an almost purplish black, and a strong wind began to lash the channels and make the waves rise in the Lagoon.

The *vaporetti* struggled to dock, and as the hours went by, the whole city emptied quickly and prepared for what she had expected for a long time but which had already changed drastically.

The big ships docked at Tronchetto looked like dangerous sea monsters as they bent to the wind that the Venetian ladies at their windows never remembered blowing so strongly.

Those who returned home did so swiftly, finding their way through the *calli* now submerged by water that had already risen a lot, looking for signs not to stumble, not to lose the cobblestones and fall into the canal.

I too was rushing home that day around 8:00 p.m. after a day's work in my design studio, between projects and concerns.

Once again, a client had criticized the renovation plan of his apartment, wanting to distort it and I, a sympathetic Venetian, couldn't come to terms with it. On top of that, my accountant had called, and a project sent in for the granting of a concession had been rejected. I hoped for a good night's sleep so I could call the next day and figure out the reason for a refusal that I found unacceptable.

I had arrived miraculously unharmed on Fondamenta degli Ormesini and opened the door to my house, finding myself in front of his dazzling yellow eyes, similar to the lights on the *bricole* that lead boats on the Lagoon at night; my cat Micio was standing at attention, sitting on the large carpet at the entrance. His two wide eyes didn't bode well, and not even my quick caress managed to drive away the feeling that something perhaps was not going to go the way we would have wanted it to and the way it usually did.

Matti was in the kitchen and was preparing our customary spritz that cheered us up at the end of the day, but that this time we couldn't sip while chatting on our tiny little terrace like usually happened on those foggy November days of San Martino summer.

As she handed me the glass, I noticed that though her hands were shaking, not even the bubbles of Prosecco that we had bought in the hills a month before were moving ... everything seemed to be standing still in an instant that would last many hours from now.

In the middle of my account of a frustrating working day, of a not so creative municipal technician and of a misunderstood Venice, sometimes even to the Venetians themselves, suddenly we heard it, strong, cold as a steel blade, unsettling, among the noises of the strong wind and the heavy rain.

That prolonged sound ... Matti and I looked at each other, stuck in bewilderment, our static eyes confirming that we were right there in a November Venice halted by that first note that marked the city like a tattoo: 110 cm.

Again ... here it was ... prolonged sound, one note ... just like that: it was not going to be a night like all the others.

I went to the window and looked at the *calle*, the lights of Paron and San Marco among a thousand drops of a rain that had suddenly become cold; in the *campo*, I could see some people equipped with boots and umbrellas struggling to move, gaining little ground in front of the fury of the wind, and the shopkeepers struggling to close the bulkheads at their front doors where the water had already entered, pushed by the wind's fury.

I was called back by Matti's trembling voice reading the news in the tide information office's website from her smartphone: it was *aqua granda* this time. Indeed, shortly afterwards we heard the echo of the second siren that, with its two sounds in ascending scale, announced 120 cm.

I felt paralyzed for a moment, frozen by an unsettling chill that was running down my spine. Venice was everything and in Venice I had everything, I had loved and hated her, blessed and cursed her ... but I had nothing else but Venice.

One more time ... three sounds in ascending scale ... 130 cm.

Overwhelmed by fear and despair, I went to the windows overlooking the *fondamenta* and, through the rain-lashed glass, I realized that the water had already risen a lot, and I immediately had the bad feeling that, although Matti and I lived in a very high part of town, the bulkhead at the entrance had already been overtaken by the tide.

Immediately I thought of what I could lose—my beloved studio, with all my projects, even the paper I was completing for the Biennale; I didn't keep copies at home, and my whole world was there ... in the tank. Suddenly everything became terribly clear: the bulkhead might not have been enough, and neither would the tank that I had wrapped in a gesture of love all over my world; my work might not have been enough to save me this time, to save us.

Matti and Micio were safe on the second floor of our building. I would have to leave them to go back immediately to my studio and try to protect what I had built in many years of sacrifices.

Matti, reading my eyes as only those who love you can do, had taken from the closet those armpit boots that I had never,

ever used in Venice and that now looked like the only way to make a safe and wicked walk to Goldoni.

I got ready quickly and went down to the already flooded ground floor. I tried hard to open the door that seemed to be sucked in by the strong wind and rain.

With difficulty, I reached the *calle,* and from there I bravely tried to move a few steps towards Strada Nuova.

I realized that many other people like me were fighting the fury of wind and rain, each directed towards his or her own little piece of a Venice that was to be saved from the fury of a high water that was definitely not like the others.

Many shopkeepers were trying to suck the black liquid from their already flooded premises, and some had already given up: by now the water was too far over the top line of the bulkheads.

Many shops had already become unrealistic aquariums. I could see everything floating inside, and I thought of the salty water eating everything, rendering useless everything it touched.

The wind made my every step heavy, and the rain slapped my face as if it were ice on my skin. Sirens chased each other, with sinister sounds of death.

I decided that the world had to see what was happening to my city, left at the mercy of the sea for decades without any protection. I decided it was time to show wounded, ill-treated Venice, so as I continued, I took a lot of pictures with my smartphone.

The trip was difficult and slow because of the fury of the storm. By that time the water had reached my knees, and I had to work very hard to locate the *calli* that had blended with the canals.

I was exhausted ... I felt drained of my energy ... I realized that two boats had been thrown onto a *calle* by the fury of the sea; further ahead at the gondola station nothing was docked at the quay. Surely the precious boats built at the Squero di San Trovaso were floating in the Lagoon with no certain destination.
I was getting closer to Goldoni when I heard what I had never wanted to hear: the last siren. We were nearing the highest level of 1966.

I could hear my mobile phone buzzing in my backpack—it was surely Matti trying to get in touch with me, but I just couldn't stop. I could now see my friend Alvise's mask shop; around that corner was my studio.

A few more steps and I saw the door, freshly varnished like the façade of the building: the water was very high, and I thought that surely the bulkhead had not prevented the water from destroying everything.

Slowly, with difficulty, I inserted the key and tried to open the door: the water had occupied the whole entrance hall and part of the staircase that served the Morosini family apartments.

As I approached the second armored entrance door, I thought about the Salute, the Lion, and the pride of the Venetians, and with my eyes half-closed and warm tears running down my numb face, I turned the key and pulled the handle slowly ....

I probably held my breath a little too long because I staggered in astonishment ... I thought I was dreaming. The water had barely reached the second bulkhead. A few more centimeters and it would have flooded the studio.

Yet inside everything was safe, all perfectly dry, not a drop of water in the tank.

A suspended world, an unreal place in the midst of so much devastation: my tank had been our savior.

I climbed over the bulkhead and took off my big boots, leaving them in a corner. I curled up on the armchair behind my desk, breathing deeply and enjoying that one minute of happiness.

The night would still be long, and the wounded, battered, tormented city would still protest for many hours and many days before recovering to a strange normality.

Venice, wounded by an exceptional tide of 180 cm, may never recover completely.

Loosely based on a true story.
Copyright CMisa (Caterina Codato).

Biography

Caterina Codato (CMisa) is an artist who lives and works in Treviso, Italy. Her artistic path began in the first decade of the year 2000 with the production of a series of watercolors realized with natural materials such as salt and coffee. Later, she attended the Scuola Internazionale di Grafica of Venice where she perfected the techniques of printmaking and of artistic books. Since 2016, she has also been involved in photography and writing. caterina-codato.jimdo.com

"We Are Here Venice: Novel Approaches to Awareness-Raising and Consensus-Building" by Jane Da Mosto, Eleonora Sovrani, and Kasia Ruszkowska

The decision to find a solution to Venice's infamous cruise ship problem was made by the Italian government in 2012, yet large ships have continued traveling through the heart of the city until the coronavirus pandemic halted all cruising on a global scale. In an attempt to anchor the debate surrounding a solution in scientific evidence, since 2017 We are here Venice has deployed an unusual "messaging channel" to provide clear and objective information on the effects of shipping: the Venetian municipality's bill posting service, alongside exhibition announcements, other cultural events, and institutional communications.

Themes have gone from the specific environmental consequences of cruise ships to more general topics like air quality and safeguarding the Lagoon. The urgent need for tighter regulations and controls on shipping traffic is emphasized throughout.

The text on the posters comes from a variety of authoritative, objective sources of information, which is then transmitted at street level to tourists, residents, workers, students, and policy makers.

Building on our anti-cruise ship poster campaigns, which have been photographed and shared by thousands of people since they began three years ago, our latest project *Back soon (but better)*—prompted by the lockdown—invited residents to remake, adapt, and illustrate posters with their visions for the city post-coronavirus.

More than 50 unique posters have emerged, each made by hand. Participants range from acclaimed artists to toddlers, while suggestions include putting Venice forward as the capital of smart working and increasing traditional rowing transportation services.

1. Since 2017, We are here Venice has used the city's bill posting service to anchor the debate surrounding the damaging effects of large cruise ships, using quotations from peer-reviewed scientific journals.

2. The simple black and white format of the posters stands out among the many colorful advertisements for exhibitions and performances that usually line the *calli* of Venice.

3. This poster reads: "The survival of Venice depends on its Lagoon system, but this has been seriously compromised by erosion from shipping traffic." Below is a computer-generated underwater image showing areas of severe erosion in the main shipping channel, caused by ship propellers and dredging.

Photograph by Eleonora Sovrani

4. In the spring of 2020, during lockdown, WahV invited residents to rework posters with their ideas about changing the city for the better in response to the huge disruption to the city's economy, which is overly reliant on tourism. The result is more than 50 unique, handmade posters, which have been put on display around Venice.

Photograph by Eleonora Sovrani

5. A reworked poster side-by-side with an original. Participants in the project could enjoy a kind of "treasure hunt" to find their own posters around the city. Each bill posting cycle lasts for 10 to 15 days.

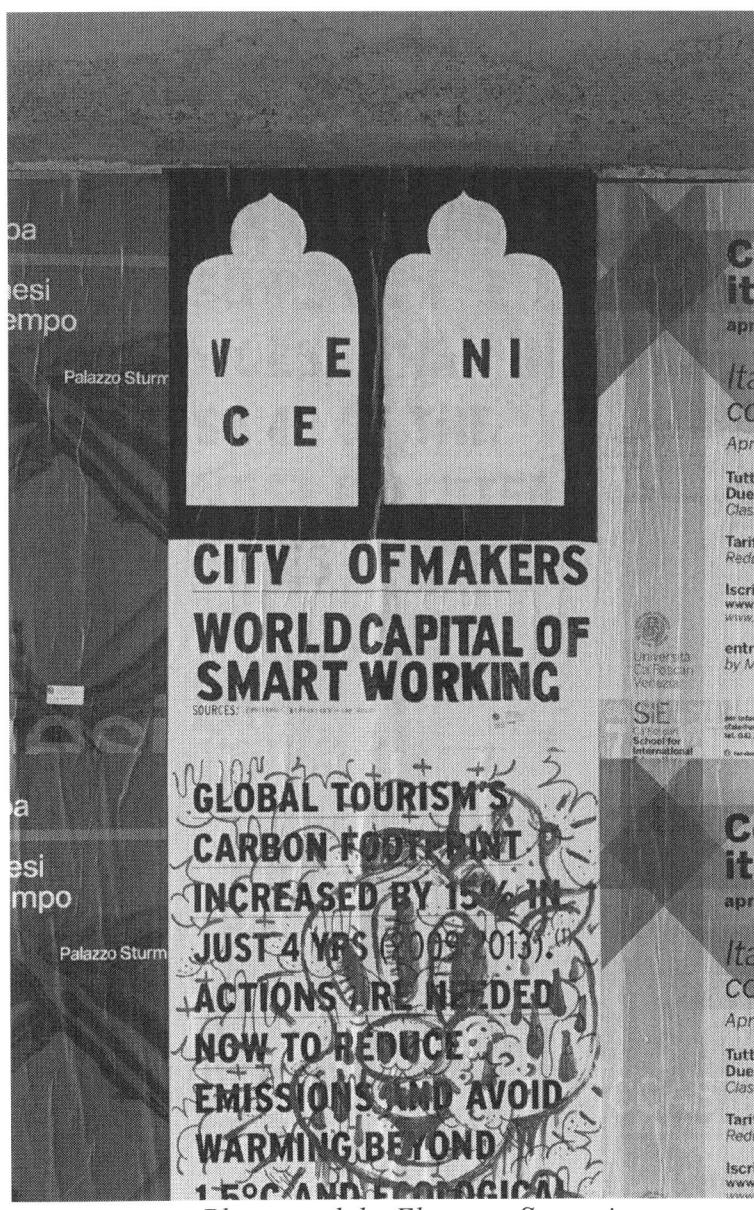

Photograph by Eleonora Sovrani

6. Among the ideas about the future of Venice, the need to attract new residents and enterprises—both innovative and traditional—featured frequently.

Biography

We are here Venice is an NGO that addresses Venice's challenges as a living city and advocates for evidence-based approaches to policy making. It works to strengthen connections between the best available information and stakeholders, collaborating with universities, businesses, cultural institutions, and public authorities to deliver projects and recommendations based on rigorous research. The aim is to promote real changes on the basis of social, economic, physical, and ecological indicators. Initiatives range from self-contained projects and exhibitions for raising awareness, to other more substantial ongoing campaigns, direct interventions, and research programs to protect the city in the long term.

"Maybe Just Maybe"
by Romi Loch Davis

much of the detritus of earlier that morning had been cleared when I ventured out for the second time on the 13th of November 2019 after the *aqua granda* ... végétal debris that the canals had spewed forth lay about here and there ... there was not the haunting corpse of a *pantegana* left ....

people were in huddles ... craving one another ....
several brought images of praying mantises to my mind ...
fatalistic resigned arms, hands outstretched and collapsed ....

everyone looked so thin ....

translucent kindness radiated through the stupor ...
some Venetians appeared diaphanous even as they worked cleaning, their essence, however, created halos about them ....

assimilating brutal adversity is chiseled into their beings ....

a couple of days later, as I returned from Murano on the *vaporetto*, mighty Venice was there in front of me ... custodian of Her cemetery behind me, sublimely beautiful, none of Her wounds were visible ...
Her millenary supremacy observing mere mortals, offering Her bounty to those She does not fragment ....

I stared at Her in awe, the east and the west, disembodied and organic, gratefully receiving the presents She bestows ... I cried

numinous Venice ....

quarantine ... *la quarantena* ... was bleak, some found it restorative.
this pestilence was all too familiar to Her ....

I sensed She was merely biding Her time ... observing, never judging ...
however, being the Serenissima, that could mean many things ....

I witnessed benevolence that shall never leave me ....

shall Venice now be purified, decontaminated as so many believe?
shall She be honored or prostituted ...
trampled over by the *mordi e fuggi*[1] hordes ...
so much goodwill is in the air ....

at present I feel Her fate lies in the lap of the Gods ....

    June 12th, 2020: Written in one bout at the end of a week that saw *acqua alta* in June, a hailstorm, and those crystalline forget-me-not blue Venetian skies, amidst announcements of returning visitors and museums opening ....

---

[1] a term used to describe "hit and run" tourism that only brings wear and tear to the city.

Biography

South African-born Romi Loch Davis worked for many years in Paris, from her first shop in the Marais and then in Saint-Germain-des-Prés. Her couture collections spilled over into interior furnishings and decoration. Couture for the house was born. Profoundly enamored with Venice as a vertiginous cultural crucible, she now lives and works there.
romi@romilochdavis.com

Photograph by Paola de Calo

"Venice, A Cry from the Heart"
by Sigrid de Montrond

So beautiful in her casket-like setting ...
She hatches every morning reflected in her own Mirror ... the Treasure Island
Not much more was needed for the placid flow to continue infinitely

On the other side of the Mirror ...
the Beauty had gone astray
Only for a while
Merely to see, She said to herself ....

Sullied Besmirched Damaged
Hunched inwards in her waters .... a minute Prince came to find Her ...
the Mirror of Lures broke
And then she cried .....

Time has passed
Her Beauty is intact
a Miracle, not a trace of a wrinkle
Barely scarred

Venice ... You could not have believed for a moment that You would drown
Nor fall asleep forever?

Life Nature Lagoon Birds have reclaimed their rightful place
And You ... defend Yourself
Awaken from your slumber
Life awaits you
We await You at all times
Imperfect and ever present
Beloved Venice

Biography

Sigrid de Montrond resides in Paris, where she and her husband Xavier de Montrond, an architect, run the Galerie Visconti in Saint-Germain-des-Prés. For over 20 years they have spent much of their time in Venice and have revitalized the Palazzo Bragadin as an artists' residence, a Biennale venue, and an event space. For her, Venice is a mixture of beauty and taxing demands that calls for never-ending reinvention of oneself with no space for complacency. Besides being a galleriste, Sigrid is a decorator and costume designer with a passion for textiles and sees herself as an "art militant."

"March 15, 2020"
by Gregory Dowling

Dr. Christian Jessen has suddenly become famous in Italy. On March 12th in a radio interview he played down the dangers of coronavirus and gave his measured assessment on the recent measures taken in Italy: "The Italians, any old excuse to, you know, shut down everything and stop work for a bit and have a long *siesta*."

Quite apart from the breathtaking racism and ignorance of this remark (as Italians have pointed out, the word "*siesta*" is not even Italian), it showed a complete lack of understanding of the gravity of the situation. My first response on Facebook was to post a link to his interview with this comment: "Send this ignorant racist idiot to one of the hospitals in Lombardy or the Veneto where doctors and nurses are working 16-hour shifts in the intensive care units at the risk of their own lives. And send him to talk to the thousands and thousands of Italians who are quite likely facing bankruptcy as a result of the shutdown."

However, leaving aside the fact that such ignorance (and racism) is inexcusable in a doctor, especially one who is apparently well-known (I'll confess I'd never heard of him until this news item appeared in my FB feed), it is true that until just three weeks ago the idea that coronavirus was not much worse than the usual seasonal flu was a pretty widespread one in Italy, too. I'll admit that, having no specialist knowledge at all, I myself bought into the notion that the whole situation was being hyped by the media, and I rashly shared on FB a video of a famous Italian art historian/politician yelling in the Chamber that closing museums and exhibitions was a criminal act. (I didn't even like this man but just happened to share his resentment against what seemed to be an unnecessary assault on culture). Most people I spoke to tended to go along with the idea that, yes, it was naturally sad that some old people had died from this virus, but that was something that had always happened, and it was absurd to start changing our lifestyles.

The fact is that when Jessen made these remarks, just three days ago, the UK was where Italy had been three weeks earlier. A doctor should have known better, but perhaps it is not surprising that many ordinary people were still playing things down. Even in this age when news travels instantaneously from one country to another, it is clear that it takes direct personal experience to bring things home to people. For some, sadly, such experience is to hear of a loved one being infected; for others it may be seeing on the news a place they know and love suddenly empty of people; for yet others it may be hearing that Tom Hanks has tested positive…. Clearly not all have yet had this direct experience. Even in Italy, doctors in Lombardy are declaring that as yet the south of the country—including the capital, Rome—has not fully taken in the seriousness of the problem. So perhaps it is not so surprising that in the UK people are still attributing the Italian lockdown, if not to laziness, at best to a southern fondness for the melodramatic grand gesture. Perhaps the numerous videos of Italians singing on their balconies (actually very moving, when experienced directly) hasn't helped here….

In any case, as a friend put it on Facebook, it's like the Renaissance: things that start in Italy soon spread throughout Europe. (Another friend added sourly that a better analogy would be the spread of Fascism.) So these few scattered notes, which I had thought of posting a few days back with the notion of letting people know what a strange experience we were going through, will perhaps instead serve as a foretaste of what will soon be the dominant style: think of it as a newfound taste for round arches rather than pointed ones, if that is of any help.

Here in Venice tourists began to disappear. In a city where people are constantly complaining about the excessive number of visitors, it was natural enough for many to see a bright side here. I myself posted not quite gloating pictures of an empty Piazza San Marco. I visited the Doge's Palace and had the *Sala del Maggior Consiglio* entirely to myself and the custodian. In the Accademia I was alone in the room with Carpaccio's just-restored *St. Ursula Cycle* for at least 20 minutes. These were undoubtedly pleasurable experiences—even if the spectral silence of the city around me was ominous and unsettling.

And now we were getting constant news reports of intensive care units in Lombardy and the Veneto being under severe strain. The percentage of those who did not recover began to grow—and they were no longer confined to old people whose health was already severely compromised. A picture of a nurse who had collapsed with fatigue over the keyboard of her computer got into all the papers and onto the TV news. Confusion raged over who was responsible for such decisions as closing schools and universities, closing restaurants and bars, stopping church services: the governors of the regions, the city mayors, or the central government?

And so just a couple of days later came the drastic decision to convert all of Italy into *zona rossa* (red zone), shutting down all nonessential commercial (and noncommercial) activities throughout the country. Flights stopped leaving and arriving. The streets emptied. Silence fell upon the cities—until, of course, the consolatory ritual of the flash mob balcony concerts started up.

That is the situation now. There is no actual curfew—you are allowed to go to the shops and even for a short stroll, so long as you do not cause an *assembramento* (crowd). Small shops will only allow one customer to enter at a time, and everyone forms an orderly queue outside—standing at a meter's distance from one another. Yes, Italians do know how to queue. All of this happened in the space of three weeks. Suddenly we—by which I mean all the sceptics and downplayers—were forced to accept we had been wrong and the "alarmists" right. If not the Black Death, and if not even the Spanish flu, this was something truly serious that was going to change our lives drastically.

Venice, of all places, should have known to take warning of health-hazards that come from the east. With its great trading networks, stretching out to the Black Sea and beyond, it was always one of the first ports of call for the repeated assaults of the plague. Two of its greatest churches—the sixteenth-century Redentore and the seventeenth-century church of La Salute—were built as thanks-offerings for delivery from pestilence. Indeed, the two most important festivals in the Venetian calendar, even more enthusiastically celebrated than St. Mark's Day, are devoted to these churches. The Venetians stole the body of San

Rocco, the patron saint of plague victims, from Montpellier in France and built a splendid church and Scuola in his honor. And as all the guidebooks will tell you, the Venetian mask with the long beak was originally a protective device for plague doctors. The Venetians even invented the quarantine system, using the small islands that dot the Lagoon as isolation units for travelers from places suspected as sources of infection.

But, of course, all that was history. Such things don't happen in the age of the Internet and antibiotics.

Until they did. Then the situation began to get very real. Speaking of my own personal experience, the first step was that the university suspended lessons for two weeks, giving us the choice of delivering online lessons or arranging to reschedule catch up lessons once normality was restored in mid-March. Which, of course, it hasn't been. Now there is no choice: we have to do online lessons—and this, for many (myself included) is a learning experience in itself. This is due to continue until at least April 3rd, but few believe that we will be returning to crowded classrooms on that date.

I myself can hardly complain. I am able to continue my job, even if in very changed circumstances, my paycheck will continue to be paid (at least, unless the Italian state goes bankrupt), and I have a fairly comfortable house full of books and equipped with Netflix (and even a sufficient supply of toilet paper). And I can write blog posts like this and catch up on social media with friends in similar circumstances.

But for many, particularly in a city where tourism is the principal industry, financial hardship and even possible ruin are not a distant prospect. This, Dr. Jessen, is not a *siesta*. And if it is a *siesta*, all too soon I suspect the UK will be forced to adopt this Mediterranean custom in some form or other. Already I am receiving emails from Italian students on Erasmus exchanges now blocked in the UK and deeply worried by what they see as British insouciance in the face of clear and present danger. They see it because they are in touch with people from their home country—and because they are not blinded by ignorant prejudices about Italians as overreacting Harlequins.

Next Wednesday I will be the *"Presidente"* of a *commissione di laurea*; this is the final academic session for M.A. students, in which they discuss their dissertations and are then awarded their degrees. This was due to take place in Ca' Dolfin, in the splendid frescoed *Aula Magna*, with its Murano chandeliers and great ceremonial mirrors (replacing Tiepolo canvases, now adorning the walls of the Metropolitan, the Hermitage, and the Kunsthistorisches Museums); the graduands usually attend accompanied by a host of friends and relatives, who then celebrate their triumphs boisterously in the nearby bars and restaurants. This time it will just be me in front of a computer and (I hope) a technician, while the other members of the commission and the graduating student join me on Google Meet. Until last week the whole commission would gather in the room with the computer and the student would be at home, surrounded by friends and relatives. Now only those relatives already living in the same house as the student will be on hand to celebrate, and the other members of the commission will join the event telematically from their own homes. I was not even intended to be the President of the commission, but the colleague who had formerly been assigned this role lives in Padua, and clearly that would be an unnecessary journey. And so I was asked to step in.

I am certainly not complaining. Indeed, I'm even looking forward to it. I will have the opportunity to walk all the way across the city, clutching my certificate declaring the purpose of my journey in case I'm stopped by the police, and the walk itself will be quite a privilege. I'll certainly walk through Piazza San Marco and cross the Accademia Bridge. There's no knowing when I'll next get a chance for such a trip.

But although beautiful in its quiet splendor, it will also be a strangely desolate city that I will be walking through.

Biography

Gregory Dowling has lived in Venice nearly 40 years. Since 1985 he has worked at Ca' Foscari University of Venice, where he is Associate Professor of American Literature. In addition to his academic work (mainly on British and American poetry), he has published six novels. The most recent, set in eighteenth-century Venice, are Ascension *and* The Four Horsemen. *More information can be found on his website: gregorydowling.com*

"Lingering at the Window"
by Maria Gabriella Emiliani

I live on the fourth floor of a very tall, centuries-old building in the heart of the Jewish Ghetto of Venice.

It takes me only 30 seconds walking to get to my workplace: I just need to cross Campo del Ghetto Novo, walk a few meters in the narrow Calle del Ghetto Vecchio, and there it is, my antique store that I run together with my parents.

I love my house, I love my apartment building, so tall and so yellowish-yellow, right next to the Jewish Museum. It has been my cozy shelter during both the last *aqua granda* and the Covid-19 lockdown. Yet no matter how comfortable it was, I could not help but spend hours helplessly lingering at the window, watching outside.

It is a demanding task to see your whole world changing from one day to another.

My windows face Campo del Ghetto Novo, which is quite a big square, where authentic Venetian life weaves together in perfect balance with tourism. If that was not enough, it is one of the few places in the world where you can experience an incredible harmony of cultures coexisting together.

You would normally see children playing soccer in the *campo*, right after school, while their mothers chat on the white marble benches, yelling from time to time in Venetian, "*Oi fioi! Ocio al balòn!*" ("Hey kids, be careful with that ball!")

In the meantime, a huge group of Israeli cruise travelers would be crossing the *campo* only to be cheerfully greeted by the Jewish community living here, right in time to honor Shabbat.

A bridge away, Ca' Foscari University students would be enjoying their spritz in the sunset light along the Fondamenta degli Ormesini, while an elderly couple would be slowly walking home arm in arm, pulling their shopping cart.

At this time of the day you would see a *gondoliere* rowing alongside on his boat, lulling a pair of lovers who are whispering to each other, *"C'était le plus beau jour de ma vie."*

This is the happiest day of their life.

It is all so perfect.

Well, it was. All of this was before.

I wish I could forget that horrible night of November 12th and the days that followed right after. We were aware that something exceptional was about to happen, yet still we could not imagine the proportion of the catastrophe.

The wind started to blow early on that evening, and it grew stronger and stronger as the hours were passing by.

As you may assume, we Venetians have always been used to *acqua alta*: we grew up with Her[1]; high and ebb tides flow rhythmically in our veins.

After hearing the weather forecast, I remember thinking, "Okay, it will be bad, we have been warned, sure, but it cannot be THAT bad, c'mon, not like in 1966. It's never going to happen again."

I feel so stupid now. I do not know why we always need to feel dismissively superior to the powerful nature surrounding us.

Right after sunset the water, blown by the wind, was nothing like the meek, gentle mass of Lagoon waves depicted by talented painters over the centuries. That night the water, our water, had become dark, threatening, wild, and impetuous.

Sirens started to spread their highest warning tone through the uproar with blasts every half an hour, meaning that the water was to increase in level much more than expected. Yet there was no way to know how high she would get.

It was clear that the situation was not under control.

Lights started flickering. Some areas of the town ended up in full darkness.

---

[1] If you are wondering, I have always imagined both water and her alter ego, the tide, as elegant, resolute, capricious ladies, while Venice, my beloved Venice, would be a charming, tired—well, now exhausted—wise old woman.

As I looked from my window once again that night, I had only one thought: "Everything is lost, and I can't do anything to make it right. My store, my beautiful store, is now under water, my precious treasures collected over a lifetime will be now floating, ruined forever. Everything is lost."

After almost 15 years in business, our antique store feels like home for my parents and me. We make our best effort to furnish it and display our items as if it were a cozy and elegant parlor to receive our friends and customers.

From the outside, because of the low ceiling, our shop may look quite small, almost stifling. Once you step in, though, you will realize that on the contrary it is a very capacious boutique, considering we are in Venice, a city where each square centimeter is a valuable resource in terms of space.

When our visitors cross our threshold, I enjoy seeing how they feel comfortably embraced by the warm colors of our Venetian fabrics, by the centuries-old transparencies of our Murano glass items, by the brilliance of our precious and rare jewels, by the vibrating spirituality of our Judaica.

"Wait a second, is this a museum?" is the question we are most frequently asked. This indirect appreciation, together with our guests' stares of awe, make every day of hard work worth it.

"All of that is lost," I kept telling myself that night.

It didn't matter that during the afternoon we had lifted each single object as high as possible from the floor, I was sure that the water would eventually either reach or capsize the supports we had used, as I was watching in terror the first videos sent on my mobile phone, witnessing the water flooding restaurants and shops not too far from us.

It is not just a question of money. We feel responsible for the past and future life of the objects we have been collecting over the years.

To give you an example, I often think of the Murano master glassmaker who, one day two centuries ago, woke up in excitement with an inspiration for a new blown glass ewer, then carefully handcrafted it with precise movements and heart pounding in his chest, afraid of making the smallest mistake. His forehead still sweating, he would have looked at the result, so happy with the elegant blue handle and the slightly iridescent body, and eventually sold it.

That ewer, so incredibly light when picked up, would later be passed from hand to hand over the decades; most of the time these objects travel great distances, remaining intact against all odds, thanks to the loving care of their owners.

Until one day in the twenty-first century, a young Venetian antique dealer would fall in love with the delicate pattern of flowers and leaflets around the ewer neck, understanding its amazing potential and bringing it back "home" to Venice.

Our job is to evaluate our findings, investigate their history, and valorize the work and possibly the memory of that glassmaker or of that silversmith, sculptor, painter, cabinet maker, engraver, micro-mosaicist, etc.

Should that wonderful ewer get broken or somewhat chipped in our hands, we would feel we have miserably failed them all.

The few steps keeping me away from my store looked then like hundreds of hazardous miles: the water was so high and the night so dark that the risk of falling and getting hurt was too great. An infinity of debris was laying on the pavement at that time, invisible in the night with the wind and water hitting your eyes.

And I decided to stay home—like many of us did, while watching from the window in terror the destruction occurring outside.

And then around midnight, everything suddenly stopped.

The wind, the rain, the water herself.

I remember this sudden, unnatural silence, this sense of immobility. And I remember the water so calm and still, laying at her top level for a long, infinite time.

And slowly, very slowly, the dark, ominous tide started to recede back to where she had come from, centimeter by centimeter.

We could almost feel the water staring at us while going slowly back to rest in her *canali*, *rii,* and *bacini*. The water seemed to say, "Don't you ever dare forget what I am capable of."

Venice did not sleep that night.

Venice stood desperate at the doors and at the windows while the water flooded Her homes, Her stores, Her offices, Her schools, Her churches, Her museums, devouring all it could.

Venice stared in terror at the cold water filtering through the pavements, mercilessly rising and rising.

Venice was alone and helpless that night.

We stayed up at Venice's side.

We held Her old, tired hands all night long.

Resting was not an option, not even for a moment.

As the sun rose, it was a new day.

Because of some fortunate circumstances, our store was—unbelievably—a miraculous survivor.

The Jewish Ghetto is one of the highest areas in Venice, and this has been of great help to all of us living and working here over the years.

Secondly, despite the intermittent blackouts occurring that night, our system of electric pumps—used to evacuate the water—worked simply fine.

When my parents and I got to the store, the day after, we almost fell on our knees in surprise. The water had made her way into the shop by filtrating from beneath the floor, but she had just got to a few centimeters high. All our precious treasures were safe and, most importantly, dry. We were among the few who were able to be soon back in business.

And we are still thankful to this day.

I wish I could tell you that it all ended that night. That we Venetians just had to clean the mess the water left, that we cried over our losses, but that eventually life went on like nothing had ever happened.

I wish.

But I cannot.

Because the water kept menacing our thresholds until Christmas, week after week. Not as high as during that cruel night, yet remarkably high, not like we had always been used to.

We were all helpless and tired. The forthcoming year, to which everyone was looking forward with much hope, was supposed to be a great new beginning in our eyes.

If only we had known.

If the *acqua alta* of November and December 2019 was a circumscribed disaster, the pandemic that has been hitting us in these months is a worldwide tragedy, seriously affecting cosmopolitan cities' health and economy like ours.

So many Venetians who were just about to get up on their legs again at the beginning of 2020, are now facing a new wave of dismay.

After the first days of Carnevale back in February, it was clear that something was off. I remember thinking that the atmosphere was too quiet, too low-key compared to the usual fresh air of celebration. The number of people crowding the *calli*, for instance, seemed to be much less than the years before.

We started hearing echoes of an epidemic in China, but it all seemed so remote.

Until the virus eventually got to Italy. And that is when our new nightmare began.

Forced to stay home, with my antique store closed according to our government regulations, I lingered at my window looking at the world outside for so long in those months.

Day after day, as the threat of a pandemic was getting closer, I saw the children pick up their ball, eyes filled with tears, and leave the *campo* holding their mothers' hands. It was way too dangerous to let them play together any more.

The huge groups of tourists went missing from day to day. In any case, nobody would have been there to cheerfully welcome them anymore.

Gathering in synagogues or in any place of worship was forbidden. Shabbat had to be honored in the privacy of one's home.

Elderly couples stopped going out arm in arm.

Gondolieri had to pull their oars out of the water and go home disheartened, leaving all romantic people stranded. The latter had no choice but to get on the first flight and head home, hoping to arrive there sooner than the virus.

The traditional places of Venetian daily life such as *calli, campi, fondamente, bacari, fonteghi,* and *mercati* were left empty. No one was to be seen nor heard.

It was like the city fell into hibernation, waiting for better times. Just like a beautiful scenography that is dull and pointless with no actors on stage to interact with it, our beloved Venice, heritage of humanity, is indeed meaningless if nobody is there to admire and share Her with the world.

Some time has passed since then, and I keep looking from my window.

Children cannot go to school yet, but they are back in the *campo* playing together. They have never looked this happy before.

People from outside Venice are not allowed to set foot in town without a valid reason, but I have already heard rumors that, as soon as possible, our city will definitely be the first destination of many.

Gondolieri, for the time being, have nobody to lull on their elegant boats, but some of them started to help the elderly by delivering groceries on their *gondole*.

As for me and my family, we are rolling up our sleeves, waiting to be allowed to open our antique store next week. There is so much to do, we have so many ideas to develop, so many people we want to meet.

All the town is abuzz like us, you can feel it, it is right in the air. Venice is finally awakening from Her fatal lethargy; Her heart is pulsing back with renewed life.

And I am sure She will be as beautiful as ever.

Venice, May 14, 2020

Biography

Maria Gabriella Emiliani was born in 1987 in a small town close to Venice; she later moved to the Serenissima with her family, never to leave Her again. With her parents she owns an antique store, Antichità al Ghetto, in the heart of the Jewish Ghetto. Her wish is for her little daughter to find in this wonderful city the very same happiness she has been cherishing for years.

"In Slow Motion, Time Expands"
by Filippo Gaggia

Dear Filippo and Views on Venice,
I just wanted to say how incredibly sad and sorry I am to hear and read of the terrible situation in Venice right now, and also to let you know that you are all very much in my thoughts during what must be an incredibly tough time.
Sending positive, healing vibes and a great big hug to you all,
Julia

The past year has sent us the highest water of the last 50 years, resulting in a huge amount of inconvenience and just as much negative publicity. We are, fortunately, prepared for this kind of event despite the fact that this time it was an ultra-extraordinary experience that shook the very foundations of what we considered a "normal" happening. The international press certainly had a field day, publishing and airing dramatic images of the army thigh-deep in water in a submerged and deserted Piazza San Marco in order to create, and perhaps sensationalize, their latest news headlines. In the days following the *aqua granda*, we were overwhelmed and extremely touched by the heartfelt messages of solidarity sent in by our clients; knowing that our loyal guests were thinking not only about the fate of the properties that many have grown to love but also about us personally, gave us strength to face the harrowing consequences that such a destructive event had on our city.

Dear Filippo,
I have just read about the dramatic acqua alta *in Venice this week. I am so saddened to hear this. I hope that you and your family are safe, and that you have not sustained damage to your home. We think of you often, and always with great affection.*
Sending love and support,
Lisa

In fact, the water damaged many of our ground floors, causing the air conditioning units and appliances (washing machines, dryers, etc.) to blow up and ruining paintwork, plaster, and luxurious furnishings. In the days following that fateful November 12, the entire Views on Venice team worked tirelessly to save as much as possible, and to say that I'm proud of them is an understatement to say the least. None of us became disheartened (although it was difficult at times!), and with our boots and waders standing deep in the salt water, we slowly worked to restore our homes and gardens to what they had once been. The submerged city was in fact at one with the sea; the water replaced the traditional *masegni* paving stones and created the feeling of a Venice moving in slow motion: wading carefully through water slows down all movement, and time inevitably stretches out ahead, minutes turning into hours.

Dear Filippo and the team,
We just got news of the acqua alta *devastation. Sincerely hope all at VoV staff are safe. While we are still considered tourists, we think of ourselves more as frequent friends. Our concerns for the staff are foremost in our hearts and minds.*
Mary and John

The slow passage and distorted sense of time was also the leitmotif of our lockdown. Covid-19 has certainly turned our lives upside down. If the high water had a significant impact on our business, Covid-19 has severely tested the stability of Venice's tourism system and almost decimated our turnover. Never before has the city been so deserted and at the same time so beautiful and magical. Indeed, we have been transported back to a time when the city lived its life in the hands of its residents.

Hello Filippo and everyone at Views on Venice,
With great hope that you are all well and surviving this unprecedented difficulty. The news in America for Italy was not good for several months but it seems as though it is getting better. Wishing you luck that, once again, Venice will rise and thrive. The spirit of the Italians, and especially the Venetians, is

unprecedented.
My heart aches to visit your beautiful city again.
Auguri e cordiali saluti,
Kathy

    … And then Venice slowly started to emerge from its deep sleep, and it was wonderful to greet clients who, despite everything and in their longing to see Venice at her most beautiful, came to visit us as soon as the borders reopened. Being able to share this (probably) once-in-a-lifetime magical experience with guests who truly love and feel part of our city has given us hope that we can continue with our work and take up with renewed enthusiasm all the special projects we had planned.

Dear Filippo,
We are looking forward to visiting Venice again soon. We are thinking of you and Venice during this challenging time and know the Venetian spirit will prevail. ❤☐
Love,
Amy

Biography

Venice-born Filippo Gaggia is the founder of Views on Venice and has over a decade's experience in the Venetian real estate and luxury rentals market. Growing up within his family's fifteenth-century palace on the Grand Canal (where he lives today with his own young family and pampered pooch "Socrates"), Filippo's expertise lies in knowing exactly what it takes to create the perfect Venetian experience.

"A Storm of Art, Colors, Story"
by Chiara Gatta

Can a physical place be compared to a feeling? Of course it can.

Venice was my home, but it was also my well-being when I was there: my happy island. It was my source of inspiration and my oxygen.

Art, colors, story, all in one storm.

The new year always starts filled with hope and new projects, but this 2020 I would say it felt surreal. Now it has been some months that I haven't lived in Venice, and I can only observe it through photos from Facebook pages and Facebook memories.

I'm always grateful living near this amazing city, grateful living and studying there, and grateful having my wedding there. But you don't realize your actual luck until you can no longer return to that something so easily.

Seeing Venice under water hurt me a lot. I saw her drowning, hoping that she would emerge. I wonder if the city can return to be like it was before, or if the damage is too great. But I love to think that Venice has passed through a lot of accidents and incidents and that this will pass, too. I always admired the inventiveness and tenacity of the Venetians, and I was sure it would be their winning weapon this time as well.

When finally I could have gone to Venice, Covid-19 arrived, a virus that has assaulted all of Italy. It was terrible. Surreal. I never expected to live through such an event.

At the time of this pandemic, I wasn't in Venice but in my city, Gorizia. I can say that at this distance I have created an even stronger link with my dear. I did not lack moments of despair, due to my inability to see loved ones. Those moments were even harder when I learned that someone lost a dear loved one. There were moments when time seemed infinite to me and others when I saw it flow too quickly.

I believe that the feeling that most accompanied me, and that managed to erase my anxiety and fears, was gratitude: gratitude for all the people who were close to me, not only physically, but also through a video call or a message in that moment. Back in my city of Gorizia, during the times when it was more peaceful, I relived moments from my childhood or from my experiences in Venice. Sometimes a perfume was enough, a song from an apartment was enough, to evoke that special place.

Biography

Chiara Gatta was born April 28, 1989, in Gorizia. Always into art, she graduated from Artistic High School ISA Max Fabiani in Gorizia and then continued her studies at the Accademia di Belle Arti in Venice, graduating in 2012 in pictorial restoration. Passionate about photography, music, painting, and ceramics, Chiara created a brand in 2014, LOVENICE, and uses it for her works. She had the opportunity to exhibit her works in Rome, Assisi, and numerous times in Venice.

"35 Minuti e sono da Te"
di Graziella Giusto

Sto seguendo dal mio isolamento, usando come tutti un anglicismo, da questo lockdown, la mia vita, come le altre in stand-by, guardo come sta andando il mondo intorno a me e osservo come da dietro ad una finestra, come da dietro la fessura di un riccio di castagna ed io chiusa dentro, giudico chi fa bene e chi no, gli esperti ci ripetono che più si seguono le regole e prima si esce, prima si esce e prima raggiungo la mia amata Venezia penso, sì perché è Lei che mi manca, perché è Lei il mio tutto, la forza che raccolgo, la mia musa, il relax, ci dividono trentacinque minuti di strada, pochi chilometri ma oggi è così lontana e così proibita che devo dimenticare la possibilità di vederla e tenerla nei ricordi come un gioiello prezioso ma dentro una teca, guardarla e non toccarla ... ed accontentarsi a sognare; e la penso futura, mi chiedo come sarà raggiungerla dopo questo esilio, bacerò la sua terra quando arriverò? E poi quali saranno le sensazioni, mi girerà la testa per l'emozione? Il suo odore mi rinfrancherà? Prima, quando tutto era normale, nelle giornate che vi trascorrevo il problema più grande erano le gambe stanche per quanto camminavo fra le calli o le ore che passavano troppo in fretta, o gli amici che non avevo fatto a tempo a visitare, ma la mia Venezia del dopo lockdown come sarà? Ed io come sarò?

Da dietro a questa finestra hai tanto tempo per pensare ma il futuro non puoi immaginarlo ora e ti accontenti del presente, il timore è che il lockdown si appropri anche della Venezia che è dentro di te, e allora combatti contro la mancanza cercandola in Google e ringrazi la tecnologia perché in ogni istante puoi scegliere di vederla, dal piatto schermo di un computer un suo filmato bellissimo, montato con la musica adatta o con i rumori naturali, o stupita vederla alla televisione in qualche telegiornale, sentire i commenti di chi ci vive quando viene intervistato descrivendola bella e splendente come non mai, che l'acqua dei canali è trasparente ed ha ripreso un bel colore brillante, dove la natura ha preso posto e si possono vedere cigni o papere, meduse e pesci a filo d'acqua o nel silenzio sentire uccellini cantare come mai visto o sentito finora ma "l'altra faccia della medaglia": immagini che inquietano, gondole parcheggiate animate solo dalle onde, campielli, calli, rive, deserti, un vuoto che agita e paralizza perché nuovo e sconosciuto! E allora basta video e prendo le mie foto, io che sorrido e dietro Venezia, io in motoscafo e dietro la Laguna ... io vicino ad un gabbiano in Riva, io felice ad una mostra ... trovo un po' di pace.

Quando tornerò troverò una Venezia doppiamente ferita, leggerò sui muri, sui portoni, il segno indelebile dell' "Acqua Alta" eccezionale di Novembre, l' "Acqua Granda," il ferro delle porte, dei rotolanti delle serrature mostreranno i danni del salso: la ruggine, ma troverò di più, vivrò il silenzio, silenzio dei negozi chiusi, nessun vociare dei turisti, nessun rumore delle rotelle delle valigie sui "Masegni," mi mancherà il zigzagare fra la gente degli uomini che spingono i carretti con pacchi da consegnare, il "Pope" "Oèh" dei gondolieri all'innestarsi di due canali, le mille sagome colorate che vestite comodamente ed armate di macchina fotografica vivono il viaggio dei loro sogni, ci sarà solo il colore dei mattoni, il bianco del marmo dei palazzi, il verde dell'acqua, ed il silenzio, assordante, e tutto questo sarà la ferita aggiuntiva nel cuore dei Veneziani, uomini e donne forti, in eterna lotta con le maree spalano fuori l'acqua, puliscono rinfrancano e ripartono, ed erano ripartiti con l'entusiasmo e la forza che li contraddistingue ma ora, il mostro virus come avrà ridotto i loro cuori?

Ed il mio di cuore di Veneziana lontana? Sopravvivo al lockdown, alla paura, ai numeri crescenti di ammalati e di vittime, alle crude immagini alla televisione grazie alla famiglia ed agli amici ma molto grazie ai pomeriggi di lavoro chiusa nel mio laboratorio, mi carico di pensieri belli, di viaggi nel tempo e di immaginario futuro, sento ancora il rumore dei flutti d'acqua di fianco ai miei passi mentre cammino veloce in Riva, tutti i ricordi mi portano ad uno stato mentale dove riesco a creare velocemente, la mia matita corre veloce disegnando gioielli con particolari già in mio possesso o da inventare, piccoli monili antichi da riadattare con "anelle" tinta oro, perline di conteria Veneziana e pizzi di Murano, costruisco facciate di palazzi sul

Canal Grande o altari di chiese da indossare al collo in Artistici Collier, ricerco drappeggi che abbiano il colore della Laguna o del Canal Grande per unirli con pazienza, tentativi, sincerità nei particolari frutto di studi su libri antichi dove scopro storie vere e leggende. Il mio cuore è fortunato, carico, la mancanza della mia Venezia mi dà forza di immaginare e lavoro, i dettagli li cerco nei ricordi, nelle foto scattate, la mia Venezia non è sepolta dalla paura, il suo ricordo mi aiuta!

Intanto aspetto, aspetto il giorno che potrò tornare da Lei, torneranno ad esserci i treni il giorno della "riapertura" delle città e per raggiungerla io ne prenderò uno, come sempre, e indosserò un vestito bizzarro già pensandomi lì, una fascia tra i capelli ed una borsa di felicità!

Ecco, anche ora, se penso a Lei mi viene in mentre un treno, credo sia naturale, è così che mi sposto per raggiungerla, i treni sono frequenti alla stazione della mia cittadina ed in trentacinque minuti sono là, e dal momento che scelgo di andarci mi sento già in viaggio, del resto decidere di partire e la strada che percorri non sono essi stessi il viaggio? E così viaggio, il treno è il mezzo, Venezia la meta!

Nelle notti insonni di pensieri e paura sento la mia città tacere, molto, il silenzio perdura irreale e, spesso complice l'aria che proviene da Nord, dalla montagna, riesco a sentirlo, un treno scorre veloce senza fermarsi in stazione, tutte le notti all'una e tredici, la prima volta l'ho sentito per caso, poi un'altra ed un'altra e poi ho cominciato ad aspettarlo, per me quei secondi di rumore di rotaie sono una specie di training autogeno, stato di benessere, chiudo gli occhi e torno bambina, quando solo un giardino ed un campo dividevano la casa della mia giovinezza dalle rotaie e dalla poco più lontana stazione e, se mi affacciavo alla finestra della mia stanza da letto al secondo piano, salendo su un piccolo seggiolino lo vedevo in fondo passare, gli ultimi metri dalla stazione li percorreva piano, e la sera, quando le carrozze erano illuminate e buio intorno, vedevo ai due lati di ogni vetro quelli che secondo me erano dei passeggeri seduti al proprio sedile, solo dopo, crescendo, avrei capito che quelle sagome un po' sporte in avanti non erano altro che le pesanti tende oscuranti in uso al tempo, agganciate con un "fermatenda" lateralmente al vetro, ma io pensavo che il treno per Venezia o da Venezia fosse al completo e tutti quei fortunati passeggeri al proprio posto che ci andavano o tornavano, e sognavo di essere uno di loro e viaggiare anch'io verso di Lei ripensando ai giorni felici in gita domenicale con la mia famiglia, con tutto quel bianco, con quei negozi carichi di souvenir, con i mille colombi della grande Piazza ... lo definisco "esercizio del cuore," infusione di benessere, ed ora mi sto trovando, a distanza di decenni e adulta a farlo, da questa casa, lontana per poter vedere i binari ma abbastanza vicina per poterlo sentire passare di notte, "esercizio del cuore" ... eccolo, lo sento chiaramente, ma che ore sono, sì, è puntuale, un pesante treno merci che passa veloce verso Venezia ... correrei per agganciarmi all'ultima maniglia e farmi portare con sè, come in un film di "007" ... anzi, volerei ... shhh ascoltiamolo andare ... 35 minuti ed è là ... 35 minuti e sono là!

Dispiego le ali come vele e complice un vento favorevole mi faccio trasportare, senza esitare, trovo subito l'acqua del Canal Grande, sembra una strada vuota ma non lo è, in esso si specchiano prestigiosi Palazzi che si ergono maestosi sulle sue rive, luccica leggero e smeraldino ed è così grande da contenere tutte quelle facciate, e lo riempiono ... Ho una buona impressione in questo momento, Venezia non è immobile, l'acqua che si muove la rende viva, ancora una volta è speciale!

Passo veloce sopra la pietra bianca del Ponte degli Scalzi, guardo la Chiesa di San Simeone Piccolo in destra con la sua grande cupola verde, incredula proseguo facilmente come in un sogno, cerco con gli occhi quello che amo vedere, a sinistra la Chiesa di San Geremia ora Santuario di Lucia, Santa protettrice degli occhi, il fondersi delle acque del Canale di Cannaregio con il Canal Grande, sento della poesia in questo, poco più in là lo attraversa il Ponte delle Guglie, quante volte l'ho passato a piedi per andare a far visita al Ghetto Ebraico ... ci sto quasi andando ma torno sul Canal Grande, mi specchio un momento, l'acqua è cristallina, cerco gli amati palazzi con occhi desiderosi, incontro la facciata Rinascimentale di Cà Vendramin Calergi, ora sede del Casinò, Gabriele d'Annunzio lo descriveva "una nuvola effigiata che posasse sull'acqua," immagino i suoi occhi e proseguo ... vedo avanti a me Cà d'Oro, un'opera d'arte, si dice fosse dipinta di oro rosso e blu poi scoloriti nel tempo, mi piace immaginarla così, e poi mi ricorda sempre un "Acqua di Colonia" con il suo nome ed il disegno della sua facciata sulla bottiglietta che mia mamma teneva sul Comò ... attraverso con gli occhi il Canale, poco più in là, a destra, i mattoni rossi della loggia della "Pescheria" secolare mercato del pesce e davanti a me il Ponte di Rialto, maestoso, illuminato con le luci dei i tre colori della Bandiera Italiana a dire "forza Italia ce la faremo," spicca l'altorilievo con l'Arcangelo Gabriele in "Annunciazione alla Madonna" e mi dona un senso di tranquillità, lo fa sempre ma ora in modo particolare ... e poi avanti, Cà Foscari con tutte quelle finestre che spaziano sul Canale, Cà Rezzonico, Palazzo Grassi ... immensi!

Alzo gli occhi, i campanili svettano, tanti, per altrettante chiese, agli approdi le gondole addormentate vestite con coperture di plastica blu si fanno proteggere, anch'esse animate dall'acqua in moto perpetuo, arrivo presto al Ponte dell'Accademia, resto a destra ... le Gallerie dell'Accademia, Palazzo Contarini Polignac e Cà Dario a me tanto cari, proseguo senza stancarmi, vedo il bianco della Pietra d'Istria dell' incompiuto Palazzo Venier dei Leoni, la residenza da viva e per l'eternità di Peggy Guggenheim e dei suoi cagnolini adorati, tutti compresa lei riposano in un angolo del giardino interno, ora museo, sembra un tassello di Lego in mezzo a tutte quelle alte facciate, e pensare quanta arte moderna contiene, ricordo chiaramente la mia tanto attesa prima visita fatta con gli amici del cuore commentando opera su opera ... Alzo la testa, mi aspetto di veder presto le inconfondibili grandi volute a spirale, ecco il barocco della Basilica di Santa Maria della Salute che sfoggia la sua bellezza, eretta come voto solenne per la peste, mi inginocchio qui alla Beata Vergine Maria, in supplica per questa moderna peste che ci ha travolti, penso forse le preghiere potranno salvarci come nel 1630, prego, ma in quel momento un lampo dorato mi distoglie, un angelo tutto d'oro, l'Arcangelo Gabriele ancora una volta annuncia, questa volta a Venezia, che la difenderà, si gira ad indicare il vento che lo spinge sulle ali: è l'angelo del campanile di San Marco, che, dall'alto dei suoi 99 metri controllerà uomini, terra e mare, mi dirigo verso la Piazza sotto di lui, è la meta, so che sono vicina, passo in mezzo alle colonne di San Marco e San Todaro entrando dall'acqua del Bacino di San Marco, ormai il Canal Grande si è fuso con queste acque, sfilo piano davanti al rosa dei marmi intarsiati della facciata del Palazzo Ducale ed ammiro i "Quadrilobi" sopra le arcate, nel mio immaginario sono tanti quadrifogli portafortuna, incontro I "Tetrarchi" impietriti nel tentativo di trafugare gli arredi sacri di San Marco ed ammiro la "Porta della Carta" appena sopra loro … mi fermo a guardare come sempre, amo particolarmente il bassorilievo che raffigura il Doge Foscari che si inginocchia al Leone di San Marco, un Doge che si inginocchia … il Leone è fiero, con il suo libro aperto mi guarda specificando il suo potere … consapevole indietreggio e mi giro … si apre Piazza San Marco, si apre il mio cuore.

Quanti giorni e sere, quanti studi ho destinato a questo luogo, ho avuto l'ardire di creare gioielli ed arte che lo rappresentassero ed ora questi studi mi sono ancora così utili che posso godermi da vicino e dare un nome, da questa mia privilegiata posizione, ai dettagli della Basilica, l'oro dei mosaici, i bassorilievi, i tabernacoli con gli Evangelisti l'Angelo e la Vergine, le statue dei Santi Guerrieri e di San Marco che vegliano sulla piazza … sfioro il petto dei cavalli in trionfo ed emozionata ed abbagliata dall'oro splendente delle stelle sul fondo blu che lo incorniciano, saluto il Leone Alato, posto proprio al centro dell'arco del finestrone centrale a sottolinearlo, con la sua fierezza mi ripete ancora una volta: "PAX TIBI MARCE EVANGELISTA MEUS" … Mi viene da salutare con un "riverisco" ed un cenno del capo, mi inginocchio a tanta bellezza.

Sono arrivata alla meta, eccomi Piazza San Marco, la meta dei giorni belli di quando bimba portavo il grano ai colombi, mi rivedo ogni volta là in mezzo! Si è fatto tardi, prima di andare però aspetto la campana di Sant'Alipio che suoni e dia il via al martello dei Mori sulla Torre dell'Orologio, prima il "Moro vecchio" che segna in anticipo di due minuti l'ora e rappresenta il tempo passato, e dopo altri due minuti il "Moro giovane" batte le ore a rappresentare il tempo che deve venire e, subito dopo voglio sentire arrivare la "Nona" del Campanile, ecco "El Paron" penso, per subito fondermi in quella nota musicale "SI": don don don …

è mezzogiorno devo andare!! E mentre massaggio i brividi ed asciugo una lacrima capisco tutto ... e giro felice, nel centro della piazza vuota, come una trottola e con la testa all' indietro, colombi spaventati prendono il volo per fermarsi curiosi un po' più in là, le braccia aperte larghe come ali dispiegate, e giro e giro, e le colonne dei portici delle Procuratie diventano le pareti di una giostra e sento la pace della certezza che mi urla dentro al petto:

VENEZIA NON È MORTA, VENEZIA SI RIPOSA!

Biografia

Conduttrice radiofonica dove prepara e scrive i suoi testi e sarta ed artigiana per creazione di bigiotteria artistica, queste sono le attività che porta avanti per lavoro e passione da sempre, questa è Graziella Giusto Madamadorè. I Gioielli che idea, sempre pezzi unici, parlano spesso di Venezia ricostruendone parte di facciate di Palazzi o particolari di arte sacra che la ispirano. I Bijoux sono spesso accompagnati, nelle sue esposizioni, da "scatole d'artista," piccole installazioni create contemporaneamente ad essi e che ben li corredano nelle loro esposizioni sottolineandone l'unicità. Chi indossa un gioiello firmato "Madamadorè" avrà "l'arte addosso." Pagina Instagram: graziella.giusto01   #madamadorèvenice

"Hymn to San Marco"
by Lorenzo Gregolin

During the week of November 12, 2019, Venice saw many days of *acqua alta*. But some Venetians took to singing! Not on that first day, but afterwards. Venetians always come back strong!

Given that we in Venice have a municipality website or an app that keeps us informed of the trend of the tide for three days at a time, we knew it would be a busy week.

The forecast for November 12 was 140 cm at 10:30 and 170 at 11:00 p.m. In fact, in the morning the maximum peak that should have been 140 cm was 127 cm, so that when the tide retreated, my partner Momoko and I went out for lunch, I think about one o'clock. That was a good day, even though it rained a lot.

We went home to our flat in Dorsoduro, near the Ponte dei Pugni. At that time I was not working because the place where I work, Ristorante Falciani near Piazza San Marco, was closed for a little maintenance. Around 6:00 p.m. Momoko went out for her tai chi lesson. But at 8:00 she called me because in the meantime the tide had started to rise, and she was stuck with other people on a bridge near the house because her boots were not tall enough. So I brought her a couple of mine. We went back home and had dinner. The fact is that, given the morning forecast, I did not believe the forecast of 170 cm for 11:00 p.m.; however, at 9:00 it was already very high. The tide level had already reached 160 cm. It seemed to me that with still two hours of growth it was understood that things would become much more serious than the forecasts had predicted.

Meanwhile, the alarm sirens began to ring continuously; in fact, in a very short time the situation went out of control. The app began to display the numbers: 160, 170, 180. Now we were in the dark because by that time the electricity had gone out in our house. The water reached over 165 cm, though in the meantime we had secured everything we could. That evening the maximum peak of 187 cm was reached; we might have had 20 cm more if the strong wind with a speed of 100 km had not stopped blowing from the Adriatic to the Lagoon. In fact, the greatest tragedy was the death of a person registered in Malamocco who, unfortunately, had gone down to the cellar to turn off the freezer but found it was already flooded.

Back to our story: we saw that the maximum danger was from 11:00 to 11:50 p.m., after which the tide went down, more quickly than usual. Then there was nothing left but to clean. Considering that the Lagoon water is brackish and ruins everything with salt, we had to clean well with fresh water. Luckily the tide did not reach our power outlets, so we could turn on the light and, above all, the heating. This was in contrast to the fridge, the washing machine, and the dishwasher, which I had to replace. The municipality of Venice reimbursed us.

On Friday, the *acqua alta* continued, with 160 cm. I saw that my trusted fishmonger had gathered his friends. The fishmongers wore their white aprons over thick winter jackets, pouring Prosecco for their friends till the bottles were empty. Over the tables of *branzino* and *sardine*, they raised their glasses and sang the "Hymn of San Marco," Venice's unofficial anthem. *"Ma un di dovemmo il suol redento abbandonar / nell'uragan pare per duol piangere il ciel parea urlar dira e d'orror il mar,"* they sang and laughed at these prophetic words about the hurricane taking the city. I watched videos of this singing from my cell phone.

Then on Sunday, at Bar Agli Artisti in Campo San Barnaba, two dozen people stood in their boots in the high water, drinking beer and wine, and they, too, sang the "Hymn to San Marco." I remember that in those days many bars and restaurants, not being able to open due to the high water, gave away wine and food to passersby. They put tables outside the premises, and people drank wine at will. *Bravi*! Riki, the bar owner, streamed a video of all the people singing and drinking, toasting to San Marco!

"Noi lo giuriam sui capi bianchi delle nostre madri, / Noi lo giuriam per gli stellanti occhi del nostro amor." In singing the "Hymn to San Marco" they all swore to protect this city, their treasure.

Biography

Lorenzo Gregolin was born in Campolongo Maggiore 53 years ago. He lives and works in Venice with his partner Momoko. Lorenzo works in a restaurant two steps from Piazza San Marco, while his girlfriend Momoko, being a native speaker, teaches Japanese at the University of Ca' Foscari. They live together in their restored home in Dorsoduro.

"V Is for Venice"
by Catherine Kovesi

As I think back to that night and the following days in Venice, three sensations remain with me:

the sound ... of a siren wailing its ominous four-note ascending scale through a vengeful wind, locked in an interminable loop;

the smell ... of putrid water in every corner of the city, ineffectively masked by chlorine disinfectant;

and

incomprehension ... at parallel perceptions of the same visible reality.

The day after the storm, I waded across Piazza San Marco, bucket and mop in hand, to assist a friend whose *magazzino* had flooded for the first time in her memory. Suppressing adrenaline and a rising tide of grief, I struggled to get past tourists relentlessly posing with smiles on their faces as they delightedly memorialized their presence in a city destroyed. Their smiles seemed ghoulish to me. Could they not see the tragedy all around? I wanted to scream at them all to put down their smartphones and help, or perhaps better still, simply to

stand, look, and weep in solidarity.

As we mopped up the filth that had worked its way into every corner of the *magazzino*, an acquaintance staying at the Gritti came to chat. Standing at the doorway, impeccably dressed, watching as we labored in the mud, she announced that she would be asking for a refund from the Gritti for the lack of room service in these days. Could she not see what I was seeing? Could she not instead simply

stand, look, and weep in solidarity?

My friend, Gigi Bon, artist, sculptor, and creator of the unique Studio Mirabilia, suffered appalling, soul-destroying damage to her workshop. Descendant of the family whose scion, Bon da Malamocco, brought the body of Saint Mark to Venice, Gigi's face of despair is also imprinted in my mind. Gigi and I had worked together on an exhibition about the fragility of Venice just one year before. Now foul water had entered everywhere—into solid cabinets with drawers full of her prints; into chests full of treasures. Perhaps of least significance was a large clam shell sitting by the wall full of shells. We emptied out the foul-smelling water inside it and loaded the shells into my Venetian trolley, or *carello*. Filling a bathtub in my apartment with hot water and chlorine, I emptied the shells into the bath. I had never realized how many spiraling crevices a shell contains until I tried to rinse those shells. The smell suffused my apartment. I can recall it still in my nostrils.

Later that evening, I walked back through the Piazza and witnessed a scene from some surreal Danse Macabre. The water was high, the lights were reflected upon it, and tourists were dancing and playing in the water as if in a flooded outdoor ballroom. A world turned upside down. Mercifully, Caffè Florian had reopened. I staggered to the back bar in my boots and drank a Cointreau as the barman and I looked at each other in shocked disbelief. I remembered Gigi's words of several years before:

"If we cannot save Venice, what can we save?"

Further heartbreak was witnessed behind high walls, in Venice's largest private garden, at Palazzo Nani Bernardo. The garden of this jewel-like palace on the Grand Canal dates back to the late eighteenth century. Its current owner, Elisabetta Czarnocki Lucheschi, has tended the garden with great care over many decades. As with all gardens in Venice, planting is of a particular type—plants must be able to withstand regular, light inundation of saltwater from the *acqua alta*, but unlike other gardens, Nani Bernardo was known for its large trees. When I arrived for tea with Elisabetta, I could not open the large door to the garden—water had swelled the wood. Once inside via a side door, she explained that the storm that night had created a mini tornado within her garden's walls. All those large, historic trees were now flattened across the carefully shaped hedges and garden beds. The only part of the garden unscathed was its little family of tortoises who had somehow survived the inundation. As I left, I noticed a stone patera with a worn phoenix on the wall. And I hoped for a little miracle.

A few days later my students arrived from the University of Melbourne. As tide after tide engulfed the city in those weeks, I witnessed their reactions as they encountered firsthand this city and its deep fragility. It was what Barack Obama would call "a teachable moment." One afternoon we stood together in the ancient Basilica of Santi Maria e Donato on Murano in the lengthening evening light as its parish priest, Don Luca Biancafior, showed us the gaping holes left in the basilica's famous twelfth-century mosaic floor. He could not use the pumps that night, he explained, as there were precious mosaic tesserae floating in the water. He waded through his flooded basilica that night, trying helplessly to catch them in his hands. In the final week of their stay, five of my students went to a tattoo parlor and had "V" for Venice pierced onto their ankles as a sign of solidarity with the city and with each other—a gesture that remains the most powerful moment in my teaching career.

Now as I sit in my study in faraway Melbourne, itself under unexpected renewed lockdown as Covid-19 cases continue to soar, I talk on a daily basis with my dearest friends in Venice, and

I sit, listen, and weep in solidarity.

Biography

Catherine Kovesi is a historian at the University of Melbourne. She has lived, researched, and taught in the city of Venice over many years. She is also a consultant with the Australia Council for the Arts curating cultural experiences in Venice for donors to the Australian Pavilion at the Biennale Arte.

"The Yellow Rose of Venice"
by Iris Loredana

The Flood – November 12, 2019

Just before midnight on November 12, 2019, the lights went out in the third floor apartment, overlooking the oldest garden in Venice. It had not only rained, it was pouring, and the power lines broke. A tornado swept across the sprawling terraces, breaking the fragile geranium and ancient pomegranate and fig trees. Down came the 40-year-old oleander bushes in their massive terracotta pots, whose rare cream and dark purple blossoms our grandmother Lina, a Venetian hotelier and chef owner since 1945, loves so much. Only a large yellow rose bush resisted, growing on top of the terrace, lovingly taken care of by our neighbors Gianni and Grazia. All year long, it acts like a sentinel, watching over what was once the oldest and largest garden in Venice.

The oleander falling off the terrace hit the ancient silver-purple rose that Lina had received as a gift from the monks of the Lagoon monastery on San Lazzaro degli Armeni. For more than 40 years, she had been using its petals to make fragrant jam, tea, and syrup.

The water was rising quickly, turning the vegetable and flower beds in the little courtyard garden into heaps of mud covered by geranium and oleander swept down from the terrace. Within half an hour, Lina's 50-year-old collection of rare Lagoon herbs was devoured by brackish water rising quickly from the ground. In other words, the loving work of our grandparents, who began restoring the ancient monastery garden plots of San Zaccaria in 1968, was destroyed in less than an hour by the uncanny forces of nature.

That night, three devastating winds clashed over Venice: *bora* (northerly wind), *scirocco* (southerly wind, bringing in the floods from the Adriatic Sea), and *libeccio* (southwesterly wind, blowing across the Italian peninsula from Tunisia and the

Balearic Islands). When these three winds meet during a tremendous storm, which happens every 20 to 30 years, they always wreak havoc in the Lagoon.

In the house, we were luckier: on the first floor, the refrigerators and other electric appliances were removed at the last minute before their sockets drowned in the rising water. Walls and carpets didn't dry properly for another six weeks, and at Christmas, you could still make out the white lacings left by the salt water on the walls.

Winter felt like Venice was finally able to take a collective break, trying to recover from the devastations caused by the flood. Homes were getting dry again, and Venetians were assessing the damage. When January came and a new decade began, many people in my neighborhood were asking themselves if this city was ready for yet another "ordinary" tourist season. What would become of Venice if this alienating form of mass tourism was going on in the decade ahead, or perhaps became worse?

We were all seeing the catastrophe approach, and we did have an uncanny feeling last summer. It started when a cruise ship crashed into the port embankment in June 2019, and the city was hopelessly besieged by tourists. And now, I'll give you an idea of what last summer had looked like from our perspective.

Overtourism–July 7, 2019

July 7, 2019, was a strange day in the Lagoon, windy and nervous, hot and cold, all at the same time. Two days earlier, an accident with a cruise ship almost crashing into Via Garibaldi had been avoided at the last minute, while a thunderstorm was bearing down on Venice, uprooting a couple of mighty pine trees in the Biennale gardens. The weather felt unstable, and the sky was filled with frizzy clouds. Harsh sun rays hit the white stones of our city almost vertically when I went for a morning walk to take pictures for my blog.

During the past four summers, my family and our neighbors in Venice had become accustomed to avoiding crowds during the day. We only leave the house in the morning for a short cappuccino break and to buy groceries. During the day, we stay inside, on the terrace and in the garden. Like her neighbors, my grandmother Lina only goes out in the evening or very early morning because at 97, she's walking very slowly and is afraid of being pushed by the crowds.

That afternoon, I couldn't resist and for the first time in three years, went out into the direction of the crowds on a July afternoon! Walking down Calle delle Rasse, I felt I was losing myself in a mighty human wave, all the people pushing their way towards Ponte della Paglia. On top of this bridge, they stopped to take pictures of the Bridge of Sighs before pushing down towards the Doge's Palace.

Along Riva degli Schiavoni, I could make out two impressive rows of 30 souvenir stalls that weren't there in the morning, selling plastic gondolas, straw hats, Venice t-shirts, very un-Venetian scarves and bags, and some of the ugliest postcards I've ever seen. On that day, I learned that Venice looks very different in the morning than it does later on during the tourist rush hour.

Fifteen minutes later, I was finally able to step into Piazza San Marco, where a few water puddles had appeared. It usually happens around full moon when tides are higher, and summer is no exception. Tourists were splashing happily in the puddles, taking selfies and pictures of their children frolicking in the dirty water rising up from the ground. *Il degrado*, as we have called it in Venice since 2014—the party was in full swing. Shivering with frustration, I found my way back towards Calle della Canonica and home, to Campo San Filipo e Giacomo where I wanted to stop for a *cichéto* and a drink. It wasn't possible because this tiny square was overcrowded, and tourists were forming long queues to wait for tables at the restaurants and bars.

In the evening, I invited friends, neighbors, and family into the garden. Journalists, writers, historians, hoteliers, patissiers, and restaurant owners, they are not present on social media, but they work hard behind the scenes, doing so much for their own small neighborhood. Lina was taking the lead in the discussion, explaining her view of what was happening to Venice, and that there was only one way to save the city. She said that very soon, the city herself would be giving a sign, loud enough to be heard, and our neighbors agreed that it would happen within the next six months. That night, the yellow rose, watching from the terrace the last daytrippers leaving Venice, looked wilted with its leaves rolled up.

The Lockdown—April 25, 2020

At noon on April 25, 2020, the bells of Campanile di San Marco were the only sound in Piazza San Marco. The Marangona bell, ringing at noon and at midnight since the year 1173, could be heard clearly almost everywhere in Venice because the city was so quiet. It was a warm and cloudless day, and I felt that we had come a very long way from the dark inferno of November and a very harsh and tiresome summer. April felt like Venice was waking up in another age.

For the first time since 1630, when the last bubonic plague hit Venice, Piazza San Marco was empty while Venice celebrated the feast of her patron saint. Only the patriarch and a handful of city representatives gathered inside the Basilica to hold the mass service. You couldn't see the Venetians, who weren't allowed to leave their homes during the coronavirus lockdown, but they were watching their empty Piazza on the webcam. Many were dreaming themselves back to April 25, 2014, when a huge *boccolo* (rosebud in Venetian) had been created in the Piazza by hundreds of people wearing red and green clothes. The rose has always been the second symbol of Venice, her peaceful and lighter face.

Spring 2020 was a strange experience none of us expected to witness: for ten weeks, Venetians were alone with their city, watching her rest, recover, and flourish. Being confined to their own neighborhood during the lockdown, my neighbors were taking to Instagram, like they had done in the summer of 2014, when the social media stage was less crowded. For the first time since 2014, news about Venice came from us, the Venetians, they said, while they were documenting the pleasure of short walks in great detail. They wrote about the seagulls leaving the city because they could no longer feed on debris left by mass tourism, while blackbirds and merlins were nesting under the roofs. Fish were breeding in turquoise canals, and even a sea horse appeared in the crystal clear waters.

The city was mirroring this unexpected change going on in Venetian hearts and minds. With tourists disappearing practically overnight, the city was slowly and painfully getting accustomed to a different way of life, and neighbors and friends became a new priority. Lina says the warning sign is here, from the planet *and* from the city.

#vogliamoriemergere–The Age of Responsible Living

Discussing the recent past and its errors while watching how the city was recovering miraculously, Venetians became more energetic despite the severe economic and financial distress caused during the lockdown: by April 2020, the city looked like one huge workshop, with residents discussing ideas for the future and ready to get started.

In my opinion, for these initiatives and ideas to become true, the government, associations, and residents MUST finally find a way to work together. There will be many capillary plans implemented by several teams. Bigger initiatives will comprise mid-term projects to bring about structural change and measures to safeguard the Lagoon. The first steps may even go in the wrong direction but may be necessary to play for the time required to implement more sustainable solutions.

As I'm writing, on June 12, 2020, life in Venice in 2020 is between #vogliamoriemergere ("We want to rise again") and #questannoèmicidiale ("This year is deadly"). The future is even more uncertain than elsewhere, but Venice could start a new cycle of life to celebrate her 1600th birthday in March 2021: ushering in the age of responsible living, while rediscovering ancient arts and crafts, strengths and stories, and sharing them with visitors, digitally and on-site.

What I learned during the past twelve months is that none of the extremes is good for Venice and her residents: the overcrowded city makes us feel alienated and sick, and the city wasn't built to be empty. We need to negotiate a balance between these extremes, and we need to accept that solutions won't come overnight, but slowly and gradually. There are always signs of hope and encouragement, if you know where to look for them.

On April 25, the yellow rose, watching over the ancient gardens of San Zaccaria, was in full bloom. It was all lush leaves and sun-colored blossoms and looked healthy like it hadn't been in years.

And then in the last week of April, a double rainbow appeared over the city, and it was photographed a hundred times. You must know that during the health crisis, the rainbow was the symbol of hope and strength in Italy—and for Venice.

Biography

Iris Loredana, CSR / Sustainability / Slow Food expert and author of La Venessiana - The Fragrant World of Venice. *La Venessiana is a slow travel, garden, and food guide, founded by Iris and her Grandmother Lina in June 2015. They show visitors the hidden Venice, never told in guidebooks, her forgotten stories, gardens, and recipes. Visit lavenessiana.com.*

"A Work with a Soul"
by Luana Segato Luse

The feeling of a timeless freedom that I felt at the age of 11 or 12 when I made my first trip without my parents, is the same that I still feel when I go painting in my studio here in Venice. I am originally from Mogliano Veneto, a town just a few kilometers from Venice, and at that age for my best friend and me, coming to Venice was like a journey for adults—it was my first independent trip, and I returned later as an independent woman painter.

I was supposed to be an assistant or a nurse or work in hospitals like my brothers, but although I did the internship and worked as a volunteer at psycho-pedagogical hospitals, I didn't follow that path. I didn't attend the Academy of Fine Arts nor art institutes; I come from the world of work, hard work, and while I was working at a car wash I privately attended the International Graphic School of Venice. The journey was long. I attended the annual courses for drawing, etching, watercolor, calligraphy, and the technique that I wanted to deepen, oil painting, for which I later worked as a master assistant. I attended various masters' studios and art associations.

I sometimes smile when I'm alone in my studio and think that, years ago, my first customer was in a car wash of a small town, when I sold paintings to an antique dealer, and now I'm here. Venice was magical when I was a little girl, and I looked at it with astonished eyes. It still is the same for me as an adult, but now I am aware of my responsibility towards it.

In this city where my maximum artistic expression takes place, it is not just a matter of creating a beautiful work, hanging it, and exhibiting it in an important art city, but it is everything that happens around it that makes the moment special: from when you head towards your studio and observe the light, the color, and reflections; its stones, its walls, its buildings; the people you meet; the smell of the rain; sometimes the stink of the sewage pipes when it is low pressure and it warns you that bad weather is coming; the scent of jasmine in the springtime; the people who greet you and ask, "How are you?" when they have not seen you for a while. When you walk under an open window and hear family conversations: *"Ti gà preparà el saor?"* "Did you prepare the *saor*?" that typical Venetian dish of sardines and onions.

Venice is unique in the world. There is no other one—it belongs to another planet. It is a poem without words that lasts unforgotten over time. When I hear people say that this city is an open-air museum, a living museum, I believe that this is a serious mistake because, if it were so, it would be like a huge room with ancient artifacts where people pay or come to exhibit their goods. This city looks at the world and needs the world to cope with its problems, but above all it needs its natives, those who were born and live here, that have given their human contribution in a timeless place where traditions are, thanks to them, kept alive and handed down. Likewise, Venice needs the art itself, because each palace, each well head, and each corner has its own particular history and tradition.

Over this past year, the city has had to face other serious problems that have challenged those who work and live there. After the *aqua granda* and during the Covid-19 lockdown, this city has rested from the mass tourism. But Venice made its presence felt more in its devastating but moving silence, and it made us understand how priceless its value is and how much it needs its inhabitants. With the support of the world, I hope the future can include smarter tourism and an increase in its residents.

Venice is not a museum—it is a work with a soul, kept open-air by its people.

Biography

A native of Mogliano Veneto, Luana Segato Luse, after her studies at the Scuola Internazionale Grafica di Venezia where she experimented with various techniques, chose to concentrate on painting, mapping out her own study and working as an assistant in studios of highly regarded maestros. In 2002 she began this journey and in 2008 opened an atelier, where she worked until 2013 when she launched her current atelier. She loves Venice's stones as well as nature and the animals. She lives between Venice and a small town surrounded by greenery near Padua.

"In the Shadow of Manin"
by Alessia Manente

Some unsuspecting Carnevale maskers are still going around unconsciously through the silent Venetian *calli,* frightened luggage is quickly escaping the outbreak of the virus, the last photoshots are eternalizing the very last moments, which are stumbling into the unknown. The ancient fear is coming back and sweeps away our perched self-confidence—a new plague is sneaking up in our lives.

Anguished groceries are swirling in the supermarkets ... the lockdown ... the silence.

Centuries-old walls are exuding consternation, anxiety, deflation: the Brownian motion of *monadi* or substance closed only within itself is now falling down into the spectral emptiness.

The dust is having a rest on the shoddy goods, in the piled up neglected Chinese bags, in the useless clothes with no identity leaning out of the dead shop windows.

Raped and abused Venice is petrified and is staring at us in her austere beauty.

A burned, steamy, stranded, exploited field, no longer able to bear fruit, is waiting frozen for its own future.

The closed balconies are signs of humanity locked in its own selfishness, its apathy, its incapacity to love our uniqueness that comes from human values: the shouted words, used, wounded, the metallic booming television voices are wheedling the hidden and frightening fears of ourselves.

Even nowadays humanity is still weak—and mortal.

Homo Technologicus is hiding itself in the virtual world: smart working, sports online, Zoom parties, Amazon shopping—remains of the fire and ashes, locked in our own homes, we are escaping ourselves.

The few people still going around during the lockdown are the poor ones: those defending their work, which hardly gives them the possibility to survive.

Check-out girls at the supermarkets, housekeeping, ACTV crew members, garbage collectors.

What am I doing among them?

Shouldn't I dedicate myself to the joy of smart working and to Pilates online?

Once Eric Kandel said, "We are our own memory."

I wish this spectral emptiness could come into my human being until it shakes me up—until it devours me into the black hole, until it washes over me, until it forces me to meditate and to let myself be born again.

I'm not afraid of the virus—I have been all around the world, I have met plenty of them, I can pull my mask down.

My body is confidently guiding my soul, opened to the sorrow of what we have lost of the past life, and opened to explore the bad and the good things waiting for me out there.

My eyes are focusing on the many faces that have surrounded my daily life and which now become a story, a friend, a smile.

Meanwhile, as I throw away my rubbish, a Veritas boat pilot tells me about himself. The garbage man calls out: "Come on!" he says, "have a good day!" The newsagent welcomes me, we talk to each other, behind the masks we become human beings, one to the other: we are on our own here, in this surreal atmosphere, a deep empathy brings us together.

Venice, place of peace and of welcomeness, heart of commerce and of culture, you are mirroring yourself in the silence, and for the first time life has left you behind.

The few Venetians are not able to cooperate all together, to give you a future and one for themselves.

Their fear is too big ... their narrow-minded egoism.

The last *aqua granda* pushed out the remaining resources. There were hands available to work and to bail out the water, to clean, to rebuild, to restart, to reopen.

I remember the first dinner in a restaurant two days after the high tide. Everything was clean, ready, fresh to welcome the guests ... the smile of the innkeeper who made it, who was on his own and who loves his work, who places his joy on the dish.

We smile, we joke, we live.

Now only the policemen are going around exercising their ostentatious and broken authority; the Hobbes ghost is showing his victory lap in the name of the virus; the civil liberties have been trampled and suspended in spite of the Constitution. Freedom of expression, of self-determination, of business ventures have been taken away; all are at home waiting for government assistance that will never come, imprisoned in an influenced and untrue reality—*non agit sed agitur*—like marionettes we are waiting for someone to move the strings of our lives.

I'm a lawyer. I can still go to my office; I travel to Mestre in an empty tram; I stand in line at the grocery store; my work is waiting for me; the courts are closed. I'm fixing my documents, and I think.

I'm alone when the sun goes down in the evening. I sit at the bottom of the Manin sculpture. I have never felt his soul so close to mine, his power in belief and in his willingness to create a world of freedom, in giving back to Venice her ability for self-determination, her love and respect for the *Digesto,* that ancient compendium of laws.

Slowly I realize that his sculpture is telling me a truth that repeats itself: "Happiness is freedom," said Pericles, who lived through the plague of Athens. "Freedom is bravery."

In the hard times we understand what really matters: I stand up slowly, and I look at the sunset that paints the Canal Grande.

Biography

Alessia Manente (12/06/1970 Venice) lived her youth in Mestre with her family; she began to discover Venice in her childhood, and from that time her dream was to live in Venice, a dream she realized 20 years ago. She restored her first apartment with love, hard work, and many friends who helped her. Alessia loves to share culture, music, and art with people from all over the world. She spends her life between her profession as a lawyer in Mestre, her passion in trips to Asia, and her adventures in restoring, in Venice, flats in such bad condition that nobody wants to buy them. She tries to give them a new future.

"Exceptional Venice"
by Fernando Masone

Reflecting on the experiences of my life in Venice and the many quite unusual periods, both good and bad, that I have lived through, these two events still surprised both myself and our city.

I have witnessed many high water phenomena across the years, yet this exceptional tide, despite the warnings and preparations, nevertheless surprised us all in its height and speed.

I had never previously worried about my workshop, given that it was slightly more raised than its surroundings and much of the city. Such, however, was the magnitude of this *aqua granda*, that I too found my rooms quickly flooded under 10 cm of water. At first thought, I was quite lucky compared to many others, yet in reality the full extent of the damage is only learned over time.

Part of my graphic archive was completely lost, along with many things of lesser value, yet all essential to my day-to-day work. Worst, the loss of so many of my zinc and aluminum matrices was of particular personal pain.

Following the floods my studio was closed to the public for many days while I put things right and returned the workshop and business back to normality. Like many, I busied myself with preparations for the new tourist season, not realizing then the coming impact of coronavirus on our lives.

Fortunately, having the studio beneath my home, I was at least able to continue my work, create new tasks to fill my time, and I finally began projects that for so long I had never had time for. Yet often I would find myself reflecting on things. The truth and reasons why all this was happening. The value of my life, and those sadly leaving us. My work, however, carried me through, even though I missed and still miss the interactions with those who have visited my workshop over the years.

In these exceptional times I have discovered Venice still always surprises us with its colors, light, and magnificent reflections. The time of coronavirus has allowed the city to reveal a little more of itself: time to study the detail of its architecture, the silent beauty of its Lagoon disturbed only by the occasional boat and the songs of birds.

Beautiful, silent, reflective.
Naked without its admirers.

Biography

Fernando Masone was born in 1952 in Pietralcina, province of Benevento, Italy. In his twenties he discovered art in Rome working at the art studio Esedra. Then in school he specialized in printmaking. From 1980 on he moved to ceramics and art prints. Nowadays he is organizing workshops in Italy and abroad. Furthermore, he is an expert in modeled art prints and special handmade paper. In 1990 he opened a lab of handmade paper, starting a collaboration with the best known contemporary artists. Cartavenezia, a gallery and art shop, was opened also in the same period, where he invited the artists who used his special handmade paper to exhibit their works.

"Tragedy Guides Us to Change"
by Marie Ohanesian Nardin

Outside my classroom window in the Venetian countryside, lightning flashed as is normal during a hot summer storm. But it was November 12, 2019, and close to 10:00 p.m. My English Conversation students and I were saying goodnight as we walked to our cars. Warm, damp wind swirled about us. The taste of sea salt in the air. "*Scirocco,*" I said, naming the south-easterly wind that blows up the Adriatic Sea from North Africa. Overhead, grey clouds darkened the glow of the full moon. *Callings of high tide.* I checked my smartphone and read the message my husband had sent me some minutes earlier: *Previsioni marea 160 cm*—sea tide predictions 160 centimeters.

Shit!

No one could have imagined then that before the night was over, the tide would instead rise to 187 cm—6 feet 1.2 inches—and leave the most glorious city of Venice in tatters.

I rushed to our home in the Venetian countryside and found Roberto, my husband and a third generation gondolier, on the couch, hunched over his cell phone. Messages pinged rapidly, back and forth, one after the other. The sender was Samuele, a young colleague of his who had been watching over the tide and the gondolas and reporting back. Samuele's 10:00 p.m. message read that the tide was high, but the gondolas were okay.

Within 30 minutes of that message, hell descended on Venice.

Samuele and three other gondoliers stood at the top of the Ponte della Paglia adjacent to Piazza San Marco's Traghetto Molo, my husband's and their gondola station. With no warning, the usually placid water of the Bacino San Marco swelled and became a raging sea. The picturesque canal that flows beneath the Bridge of Sighs and below the bridge the men were standing on, burst into a rushing river. Waves crashed over the marble balustrades, and the tide rose at them from both sides of the bridge. Water taxis, *vaporetti,* and gondolas were thrashed about.

Maria, my husband's gondola, had been ripped from her docking spot. Desperate, and from the bridge, the men tried to lasso *Maria*—the way ranchers would dominate a wild horse. They had to save her from crashing against the stone embankment—or worse, against the bridge.

All the while, we received terrifying messages and video clips of the storm from Samuele, friends, and other colleagues. The high tide, now a series of violent waves, rushed through the city. Shocking for us from the security of our home, it was horrific for the gondoliers who were determined to save Roberto's gondola. Their struggle to keep *Maria* from being destroyed continued as the sea roared, and the high tide rose to the second highest level in recorded history. But their attempts became dangerous for them—and futile for *Maria*. The wind roared at 100 km/h. Stuck at the top of the bridge, the men had no choice but to hold on tight. My heart dropped as my husband yelled through the phone, "Let her go. *La barca* can be replaced, you guys can't."

Only then, and by the grace of God, the wind and tide shifted and pushed *Maria* against a shattered lamppost at the foot of the Ponte della Paglia. Battered and beat up but in one piece, she was miraculously left there and under the watchful eye of the *Madonna dei Gondolieri*, the sixteenth-century bas-relief sculpture and protector of gondoliers that decorates the façade of that bridge.

As these events unfolded into the night, I dutifully sent the breaking news to the American news agency producers I collaborate with. In the past months and years, I had worked with them on stories in Venice that covered high tide, overtourism, and the cruise ship accident. As serious as those stories were, and remain, they couldn't compare to the devastation that was occurring that night.

It pained my husband not to be in Venice to care for *Maria*. He wanted to go, but I insisted, before I demanded, that he wait until the storm passed—which it did as quickly as it arrived. After midnight, Roberto met his colleagues at the entrance to Venice. They pulled on their boots and began what under normal circumstances would be a 15-minute walk to Piazza San Marco. Walking in knee-high water in the dark, the *passegiata* took them close to an hour. The only light they had came from their smartphones. No electricity. No dry spots. Water and debris in every direction. Anyone who didn't know the nooks and crannies of Venice would have ended up, possibly drowning, in one of her canals. When they arrived at the Traghetto Molo, the tide had receded enough for them to secure *Maria*. They rested her on the trestles of the high water walkways or *passarelle*. She would be safe there until morning when Roberto could return and assess the damage.

It was 4:00 a.m. when Roberto returned home, and we turned off the light. A few hours later my phone filled up with responses from the American news agency in London and Rome. A news crew was on their way. While I worked the phone between the producers and organized interviews with those effected by the exceptional high tide, Roberto returned to Venice to tend to *Maria.*

He arrived in Venice by 10:00 a.m. The tide had yet to fully recede. Wearing knee-high boots, he searched specialty stores for waist-high waders. The town's supply was already depleted. At the Ponte dei Bareteri, the rising tide forced him to wait. He couldn't go any further, nor get to *Maria*. Frustrated at the top of the bridge, he received photos and videos from his colleagues of the damage his gondola had sustained. Thankful she could stay afloat and that the damage was repairable, Roberto's colleagues stood in thigh-high water and guided her, with the care one would handle a newborn, to a safe docking spot.

Late that afternoon when I met the Rome news Bureau Chief at the Santa Lucia train station, the tide had receded once again. We shot a piece for the evening news and then went to our hotel. The remainder of the crew would arrive late that evening by air from London.

The hotel, spotless and clean only hours after it had been flooded, was not running full service. The elevator had been damaged, so I took the stairs to my second floor room. At dinner time the concierge, desirous to assist, couldn't direct us to an open restaurant. The city had shut down. Still, hunger pushed us outside. We walked through the dark, damp city, twisting and turning down *calle* after *calle*. Our quest to quiet our growling stomachs began to look hopeless. Then, in Campo Santo Stefano the pizzeria lights spilled out onto the wet pavement. *Yes!* Instead, no. Being one of only a few places open in a town full of tourists to feed, there was no room for us.

Across the *campo*, a waiter was opening the doors to Ristorante A Beccafico. We rushed over, walked up the marble step entrance and into the empty restaurant. We were seated immediately. Our table was set with white linens, silverware, wine glasses, and a lit candle. But the elegance of the dining room couldn't hide the dampness on the stone floor beneath my feet. The waiter was pleasant, tried, and tired. When I asked how they had been impacted by the high tide the night before, he pointed to the waterline mark on the wall. It stood as high as the table top. After a night of terror, and a full day of cleaning and drying out the dining room and the kitchen, they decided to carry on and open the restaurant. My stomach was thankful for their decision.

While the restaurant filled up with patrons speaking diverse foreign languages, my colleague and I discussed the news story over a glass of ruby-red Valpolicella wine and waited for the bread basket that didn't arrive. Sometime later, and after our third request for bread, the waiter appeared with a basket of warm, sliced baguettes. His smile apologized for making us wait. He explained that the tide had damaged their oven. They couldn't bake or warm up their own bread, or serve anything on the menu baked in the oven. He had gone to the neighboring restaurant to get bread solely for our table. His energy, kindness, and intent to please under such dire circumstances had me apologize for not having considered the difficulties they faced. Grateful for his effort and the warm bread, my colleague and I enjoyed stovetop-grilled beef fillet and vegetables and, of course, the wine.

The next morning the sun was out, and the weather was calm. The tide had normalized but was expected to rise again in the next few hours. Our boat driver took the crew and me down the Grand Canal, across Bacino San Marco to the Castello district. Under a brilliant blue sky, Venice was a theater of war. Dozens of gondolas, toppled and scattered about like toothpicks, lay on dry land. Water taxis, ripped by the wind and water from their mooring spots, blocked narrow pedestrian *calli*. *Vaporetti*, waterbuses weighing over 27 tons each, sat on the stone pavement or on each other; the sterns of the boats stuck up in the air, the prows under water. Glass store fronts and luxury hotel windows were shattered. The contents of ground floor spaces in town lay soaked in sea water, waiting to be thrown out.

At the entrance to Via Garibaldi, the main pedestrian street lined with bars, shops, and restaurants in the populous Castello district, we spoke to the owners of the Domino Arte antique shop. Two nights earlier and during the storm, a six foot tempestuous river of sea water had raged through the wide stone *via*, disintegrating the store front window of the family-owned business and turning the below-street-level shop into a water well. Precious antique side tables, chairs, lamps, and memorabilia floated about. Seeing the devastation to this and every shop, restaurant, home, church, business, or storage space at ground level in the city was difficult to digest, yet real. The financial loss incalculable. The solidarity and Venetian determination palpable. Clean up began the moment after photos were taken. Neighbors helped neighbors as the tide rose again.

Morning and night for the next three days, flood sirens that resemble air raid warnings followed by a series of escalating tones alerted the city of the return of exceptional high tide. Once again, the tide prediction was 160 cm. The Mayor closed Piazza San Marco off to the public. Only shop owners, the press, and government officials were allowed access. Working in the wind and rain, and in hip-high, cold sea water we, and every major news agency in the world, spoke to any shop owners or cafe managers who weren't too tired or defeated to talk with us.

Financial loss and emotional devastation crushed the city residents and business owners. A sense of defeat was expressed by some, while the determination to not give up was voiced by the majority. Still, no one hid their fear of future exceptional high tides. Nor did they hide their anger at the decades of corruption that surrounded the billions of euros spent over three decades by local and national administrations, and the false promises to protect Venice from succumbing to a similar or lesser high tide.

Through the winter months, the aftermath of water damage affected all who live or work in Venice. The promise of government aid provided hope and some relief. But tourism, Venice's top economy, suffered the most. Tourists didn't understand that the November tides were exceptional. They seemed to believe that Venice remained under water, and they canceled their travel plans.

In February, to the delight of those whose livelihood depends on tourism, visitors returned for Carnevale. The city's *campi*, the Piazza, restaurants, cafes, and hotels filled with masquerading guests and locals, music, and celebration. Foreign visitors, dressed in elaborate costumes, attended balls in luxurious palaces. The government and private funds began trickling in to aid and reimburse residents and business owners for damage expenses related to November's high tide. Mere months before Carnevale, the Venetians had been financially and emotionally knocked to their knees. Then, as the city was getting back on her feet, Covid-19 arrived and landed the final blow.

Carnevale celebration was canceled the day before *Martedì Grasso*—Fat Tuesday. By the end of that same week, Venice resembled a majestic ghost town. What had been labeled a bad flu began infecting thousands and taking hundreds of lives in Italy. Travelers who planned to visit Venice and elsewhere in Italy during 2020 got nervous. Reservation cancellation numbers escalated, too.

In early March, when the Italian national government declared a countrywide lockdown, we stayed home. My husband left our home once every two weeks, and only for grocery shopping and pharmacy runs. He wasn't permitted to leave our countryside town and go to Venice. Not even to check on *Maria*. Except for open-air walks with our dog, which were restricted by law to a 200-meter radius from one's residence, I never left my home.

But peace fell over the country. Planes stopped flying. Cars remained parked. Trains and trucks reduced their number of journeys. Fish and wildlife moved about more freely. Spring glistened, and the sky turned bluer than blue. Dogs barking, birds chirping, and neighbors singing from balconies displaying rainbow drawings that read *"Andrà Tutto Bene"* or the Italian *tricolore* flag became familiar sounds and symbols. The nightly Covid-19 report made us shudder as the numbers went up. We disinfected and washed our hands, baked cakes and lasagnas, mixed Aperol or Campari spritz *aperitivi,* planted our first vegetable garden, terribly missed seeing and hugging our daughters, said goodbye to our dog, Bacco, who died in the midst of the pandemic, and sadly learned of the death of a friend, and that of friends of friends to Covid-19. Italy and Italians, known for creativity more than discipline, pulled together and behaved admirably. The general population's health and well-being came before the personal and economic sacrifices, which continue to be felt. As hard as the economy has been hit, the Covid-19 infection rate curve in Italy has been flattened. Now, wearing masks and social distancing, we plan to keep it that way.

In less than one year, Venice succumbed to the *MSC Opera* cruise ship crash, a season of overtourism never seen before, the second highest tide in recorded history, and Covid-19. Life tosses us tragedies to guide us to change our ways. These events are warnings. Mother Nature, a higher power, simple common sense, or all of these together are screaming loud and clear for sustainable change in Venice and around the globe.

What comes next? Will the multitude of small businesses, artisans, and independents that rely on tourism survive 2020? Will a vaccine arrive in time for 2021? Will tourists return in the unsustainable numbers that were? Or will local and national administrators together with the tourism industry utilize this slowdown period to plan for a more sustainable future?

We have been given the signs. Collectively, we must find the courage to listen to them and make the changes.

Biography

Marie Ohanesian Nardin was born in Los Angeles, California. A former banker, she is the author of Beneath the Lion's Wings, *a novel set in Venice, Italy. She collaborates with various news outlets and lifestyle production companies from the United States, Canada, Italy, and the United Kingdom. The mother of two daughters, she has lived in the Venetian countryside with her husband for over 30 years. MarieOhanesianNardinAuthor.com*

"Exploring the Silver Lining of Adversity"
by Liesl Odenweller

Most Venetians or Venice lovers know exactly where they were, and what they were doing on the evening of the *aqua granda*. I happened to be at Penn State University, rehearsing for the inaugural concert of Venice Music Project's first US Tour. You can imagine the consternation and distress that we all felt, rehearsing and performing a program of Venetian music, taken from a manuscript that musicologist and PSU professor Marica Tacconi had discovered in the Marciana Library the previous year, while this unprecedented disaster was sweeping through Venice.

The entire audience joined us that evening in weeping for Venice, as the photos and videos kept coming through, and this solidarity continued throughout our tour. While we all missed the worst of the flooding, very high tides continued two weeks later when we returned and well into December. Our newly rented ground floor office had been under over a meter of water and ultimately was not salvageable. St. George's Anglican Church, where VMP holds its Venice concerts, had been flooded by 30 cm of water, unheard of since 1966. Multiple friends' businesses, suffering through the onerous and costly cleanup after each new high water, were on the verge of bankruptcy by the end of 2019.

And yet 2020 began with a sense of great promise and renewal. Then Covid-19 hit.

For Venice Music Project, the nonprofit that I helped create in 2013 and continue to run, it meant canceling the opening concert of Season 2020, slated for March 1. And then the second concert on March 8. Eventually, we resigned ourselves to canceling the entire first part of Season 2020, up to the end of June. My team and I had worked so hard to create an interesting and innovative new season, and we were to welcome two young, promising singers for a concert of arias and instrumental music from G.F. Haendel's *Giulio Cesare* as our opening. Other works to be presented in the first part of the season were some of the

"Hidden Treasures" discovered during VMP's musicians' musical archaeology in archives in Venice; Nicolo' Jommelli's haunting *Requiem* with renowned choral conductor Tim Brown joining us with a chamber choir from the UK; and programs dedicated to musical voyages between Venice and other European cities, among others. We had engaged 14 musicians and five singers for the course of the Spring Season, all of whom were suddenly out of work, with no safety net—ourselves included. It was devastating.

Yet while all of that was going on, we were going into lockdown, and I was forced, for the first time in years, to take a step back from my normally frenetic life. There was a bizarre contrast between feeling a panicked need to keep working and taking care of the musical family that I feel responsible for, and having no choice but to slow down. For the first time in my life, I wasn't exhausted by the time Easter Sunday arrived, having rehearsed and performed incessantly during the preceding weeks. I suddenly found time to read, take an occasional nap, start sleeping properly at night, finish moving into our new home, and plant a vegetable garden. Who knew if the food supply chain would be affected?

Living with a view of the Giudecca Canal and slowly watching the water become calmer to the point of eventually seeing quite evocative reflections of San Giorgio Maggiore and the Salute was enchanting. I never found Venice sad or abandoned, but rather more beautiful than ever, and I rejoiced at being the only person on the street (and felt safer, too!). Birds and fish that we normally saw in small numbers became ever-more abundant. I felt privileged to see and photograph my beloved city in this special moment.

My husband, who normally travels almost every week for work, was home for the duration. My daughter, who is nearly 17 when I write this and attends a local Liceo Classico, was doing her school online. We cooked more elaborate meals than usual and spent precious family time together. I took advantage of the unexpected freedom to catalogue piles of music, learn new arias, think of new programs, and start teaching myself to play the harpsichord. Inspired by Giovanni Boccaccio's *Decameron*, I also launched *21st Century Decameron* to help people to share their quarantine stories, photos, and experiences.

At first, we were terrified to even leave the house, but obviously groceries quickly became a necessity. We live on the Giudecca, and just taking the *vaporetto* to the Zattere became an immediate challenge. At the beginning of lockdown, there were very few boats, and only as a ferry between the Palanca and the Zattere about once per hour. People were not too clear on the ramifications of social distancing, and I was grateful to have my shopping cart with me to help enforce it. I decided to fill out my declaration paper in its various iterations and risk my normal trek to the organic supermarket near Campo San Luca and the organic market near Piazzale Roma, just to get out and walk a bit in the fresh air. This also became my only opportunity to see friends: we would stand two meters apart and mime giving each other hugs, then walk toward our destination, always masked and socially distanced, and chat until we needed to go our separate ways. Every time I saw police, I smiled and greeted them, but I was never stopped and asked for my papers, although other friends were.

Shortly after the lockdown began, Venice Music Project received a request from Monteverdi Tuscany, the beautiful boutique hotel in southern Tuscany where we perform several times a year: to entertain their clients during lockdown, they had created "*La Bella Musica di Monteverdi Tuscany*," a platform on their website with socially distanced performances by some of the musicians who have performed for them over the years, and we were asked to contribute. Other performers, particularly those in the New York area, were able to receive delivery of properly sanitized professional recording equipment. Since in Venice we risked enormous fines if we left our homes for all but essential errands, three VMP musicians taught ourselves the technology and recorded the most authentically socially distanced music video of their collection so far, of three songs by Claudio Monteverdi, filmed separately from each of our homes and put together with an app.

Once that was accomplished, I needed another project to keep me sane, so I started working toward organizing a live-streamed concert once the lockdown finished and VMP could once again be in the same space and make music together, even without an audience. We finally achieved this on Sunday, June 28, with the generosity of some of our supporters and the kind hospitality of Filippo and Rachele at Views on Venice. Despite technical difficulties from the hosting platform's side, we had an audience of over 200 people all over the world, which was quite exciting!

In the meantime, my daughter finished her school term. Despite her frustration with the challenges of learning online, she worked incredibly hard and finished up satisfied with her effort and the results she achieved. My husband launched an online course that he had never had time to finish preparing before, in addition to helping some of his clients remotely.

Today, as I write this, is the Festa del Redentore, the celebration of the end of another pandemic. Last night's fireworks were canceled, purportedly to avoid crowds, although the masses of people present on the Giudecca until the early hours of this morning, mostly without masks anywhere in sight and crowded together with no thought of social distancing, are an unfortunate testament to the city's lack of commitment or ability to actually enforce the current regulations.

I have to admit that I continue to wear a mask whenever I am out, unless I am outdoors and there is absolutely no one in sight. I have no intention of setting foot on a train or airplane any time soon, much as I desperately want to visit my aging parents in the US. I get very nervous in large gatherings and go out as little as possible. I have nothing but esteem for Italy's initial handling of the pandemic, but I fear that things have become a bit complacent and careless in the reopening. Venice's *centro storico* only had about 40 cases of the virus, but with all the people now coming in from around Europe and not respecting (or, to be fair, even being asked to respect) any of the restrictions still theoretically in effect, I fear it is only a matter of time until we find ourselves in bad shape again.

In theory, Venice Music Project could start holding concerts again. St. George's is uniquely predisposed to flexible seating with social distancing, and as a classically trained singer, I actually expel very little air when I sing and present little risk for potentially infecting anyone. But we prefer prudence and will wait at least until the Autumn to see how things go. When the time comes, we will carefully evaluate risks and enforce all safety precautions. We are all eager to start sharing our music again, but perhaps we will need to focus on more live-streamed concerts rather than live ones.

I wish that I could share evidence of an epiphany on the part of the city and most of her residents, and a resolution to reshape Venice's future reality following these two major disasters, but aside from a few small new initiatives in addition to the already existing ones, I see very little evidence that most people are doing anything further than desperately hoping everything will go back to "normal" as soon as possible. As a noncommercial, nonprofit organization that welcomes, but does not depend on, visitors, Venice Music Project continues to research and preserve the great tradition of Venetian baroque music, much as other organizations restore Venice's art and monuments. Our mission will continue no matter what else happens to the city, even if we are unable to hold live performances of our discoveries. But we are a very small minnow in that large sea of commercial interests.

Community has always been important in Venice, and these times have been no different. Helping others around us both helps them and comforts us. And helping others is the way forward that seems to make the most sense on every level. Venice's residents sadly form only a small community, but we are fortunate to have daily contact with many friends and neighbors on the streets. Since this was largely missing during the lockdown, the intense joy of encountering even someone we only knew by sight was and still is unexpected and keeps me smiling for hours afterward. Everyone I know took groceries or extra food or home-baked goodies to others. Many started collecting donations of food and money to purchase groceries for those in need. My daughter frequently took samples of our Covid baking to the homeless man who lives on our *vaporetto* stop. St. George's began holding Zoom church services, which will continue until the Fall, when we hope to hold services in the church once again, while still offering the online option to those at risk or far away. That community has also been of great comfort.

In terms of my family, as the situation worsens daily in the US, I desperately wish that I could bring them here. I can only hope that they will stay healthy. Being an expatriate is wonderful in so many ways, but this is a terrible time to be cut off from and unable to help loved ones. So please, everyone, stay safe and healthy. We want to see all of you in Venice again soon.

Biography

Soprano Liesl Odenweller is a cofounder of Venice Music Project, which supports musical archaeology in archives all over the world to restore and share the amazing musical treasures from the Venetian baroque period. She also performs in opera houses and with important orchestras and conductors in Europe and the US. venicemusicproject.it

Photograph by Katharina John

"Non È Facile"
di Paolo Olbi

Non è facile per me raccontare questi avvenimenti così disastrosi. Io ho già vissuto questa triste esperienza che travolse l'intera città nel novembre del 1966, isolandola completamente. Mancava la luce e non si poteva uscire dalle case, né comunicare. L'anno prima era morto mio padre e già questo era stato per me un trauma.

Quando finalmente si poté uscire andai ad aprire il mio laboratorio, era un magazzino di due stanze di 17 metri quadrati ciascuna. L'anno precedente avevo firmato parecchie cambiali per poter avere le macchine indispensabili per iniziare l'attività di legatore di libri, e con questo finalmente realizzavo il mio sogno di lavorare in proprio.

Quella mattina del 1966 feci molta fatica ad entrare perché l'acqua aveva invaso per 90 centimetri il mio laboratorio rovesciando i mobili in legno e i tavoli da lavoro con tutto il loro contenuto. L'acqua, scendendo, aveva trascinato con sé tutto il materiale verso l'uscita, ostruendo l'accesso al laboratorio. Riuscii ad entrare solo con l'aiuto di un amico.

Una volta entrato, accesi una candela e al suo lume traballante mi si presentò il disastro in tutta la sua realtà. Cominciai a camminare su carta, cartoni, attrezzi… il pavimento era completamente coperto di fango, acqua di fogna e gasolio uscito dalle caldaie per il riscaldamento. A fatica ho trattenuto il pianto, avendo appena finito di pagare quella merce e i macchinari. Tutto era distrutto, tutto era rovinato. Bisognava ricominciare da zero, avevo perso tutto.

Pensai che mai più avrei vissuto un simile disastro per la mia attività.

Purtroppo mi sbagliavo perché nel novembre del 2019 ho rivissuto questa esperienza.

Nel 2018 mi ero proposto di insegnare il mio mestiere a dei giovani che avessero la mia stessa passione. Negli anni trascorsi la mia attività si era ampliata: non solo legatoria ma stamperia, cartotecnica e altre attività inerenti al libro. Avevo anche organizzato a Ca' Zenobio, una volta Collegio Armeno ora dismesso, quattro bei laboratori che affrontavano i vari aspetti del mio lavoro.

Si sono offerte di imparare due ragazze molto brave: Anna diplomata all'Accademia di Belle Arti di Venezia ed Elena laureata nella Conservazione dei Beni Culturali. Le mie allieve erano molto contente perché vedevano nell'evolversi delle cose un buon futuro di lavoro.

Il loro entusiasmo però è finito nel novembre scorso perché ci siamo ritrovati con lo stesso problema del novembre del 1966. Dopo cinquantatré anni, il disastro si è ripetuto e ci siamo ritrovati di nuovo con 90 centimetri d'acqua. Il negozio era appena stato allestito con gli articoli di carta e di pelle della nostra produzione: album foto, diari, cartelle scatole e altri oggetti di nuovo immersi nell'acqua e nel fango. Le cassettiere con i caratteri mobili della tipografia sono ancora oggi da aprire e lavare per salvarli dall'ossido di piombo. Metà del patrimonio del nostro lavoro è da buttare!

Anna e Elena sono desolate perché dobbiamo ricominciare tutto da capo, buttando e ripulendo ogni cosa, io cerco di incoraggiarle avendo già vissuto quel disastro. Cominciamo a rimettere ordine sostenuti dal fatto di essere stati selezionati per partecipare con i nostri prodotti all'esposizione "Homo Faber" della Fondazione Michelangelo, coscienti che per noi sarà un rilancio, ma due mesi dopo arriva la pandemia vanificando ogni nostro sforzo con blocco totale delle attività.

A sei mesi dall'aqua granda ancora viviamo nell'assoluta mancanza di possibilità per il nostro lavoro e nell'incertezza del futuro. Ho addirittura consigliato alle mie allieve e collaboratrici di trovarsi un lavoro più sicuro rispetto al lavoro autonomo, che è garantito solo dalla volontà dell'imprenditore-artigiano, troppo soggetto alle crisi economiche che si ripetono ormai periodicamente e all'avversità e al silenzio delle autorità che molto spesso vedono nel lavoro autonomo una fonte di lavoro in nero. Questo è quanto mostrano i cartelli "Cedesi attività" esposti da moltissimi negozi.

Per quanto mi riguarda, dopo 60 anni di lavoro mi ritrovo costretto alla resa: è finito il sogno di una Venezia viva di giovani artigiani che con le loro attività e la loro bravura potessero contrapporsi alle grandi firme e alla paccottiglia che invade la città.

Venezia 23 giugno 2020

"It's Not Easy"
by Paolo Olbi

It is not easy for me to recount these events, so disastrous. I have already lived this sad experience that swept the whole city in November 1966, isolating it completely. There was no light, and you could not leave the house or communicate. The previous year my father had died, and this had already been traumatic for me.

When I was finally allowed out, I went to open my laboratory. It was a warehouse of two rooms, 17 square meters each. The year before I had paid several bills in order to have the essential machines to start the bookbinder business, and with this finally fulfilled, my dream of working on my own came true.

But on the morning of the *aqua granda* I had a hard time getting into the warehouse because the water had invaded my workshop up to 90 cm, overturning the wooden furniture and work tables with all their contents. The water, going down, had dragged all the materials through the exit, obstructing its access. I was able to enter only with the help of a friend.

Once inside, I lit a candle, and in its rickety light, the disaster in all its reality presented itself to me. I started walking on paper, cardboard, tools ... the floor was completely covered with mud, sewage water, and diesel fuel coming out of the boilers. With difficulty I held back the tears, having just finished paying for the goods and the machines. Everything was destroyed, everything was ruined. We had to start from scratch. I had lost everything.

I thought that never again would I experience such a disaster for my business. Unfortunately I was wrong because in November 2019 I re-experienced this event.

In 2018 I had proposed to teach my craft to young people who had the same passion. In the past few years my business had expanded, not only bookbinding but printing, paper making, and other activities related to books. I also organized four beautiful workshops in Ca' Zenobio, once an abandoned Armenian College, which dealt with various aspects of my work.

Two very skilled women offered to learn: Anna had graduated from the Accademia di Belle Arti di Venezia, and Elena had graduated from the Conservazione dei Beni Culturali. My students were very happy because they saw a good working future evolving.

Their enthusiasm, however, ended last November because we found ourselves with the same problem as in November 1966. After 53 years, the disaster had repeated itself, and we found ourselves in 90 cm of water. The shop had just been set up with paper and leather goods we had produced: photo albums, diaries, folders, boxes, and other objects—but again water and mud were everywhere. The chests of drawers with the movable characters of the typography are still to be opened and washed to save them from lead oxide. Half the wealth of our work, to be thrown away!

Anna and Elena were desolate because we would have to start all over again, throwing away and cleaning up everything. I tried to encourage them, having already experienced this disaster. We began to restore order, supported by the idea that we had been selected to participate with our products at the exhibition of "Homo Faber" at the Michelangelo Foundation, aware that for us it would be a revival. But then two months later the pandemic arrived, frustrating all our efforts, with a total blockade of every activity.

Six months after the *aqua granda*, we still live in the absolute lack of possibilities for our work and in the uncertainty of the future. I also advised my students to find a safer job than self-employment, which is not guaranteed just by the will of the entrepreneur-craftsman, who is too subject to the various economic crises that are periodically repeated and to the silence of the authorities who see self-employment, very often, as a source of undeclared work. This is what the *"Cedesi attività"* (going out of business) signs displayed in many shops show.

As for me, after 60 years of work I find myself forced to surrender: my dream of a Venice has come to an end, once alive with young artisans who with their activities and their skill could contrast with the big names and the junk that invades the city.

Venice, June 23, 2020

Biografia

Paolo Olbi è nato a Venezia il 23 ottobre 1937. In gioventù ha rinunciato a un lavoro "sicuro" come impiegato dipendente per seguire la sua passione per la rilegatura dei libri. Autodidatta, aprì il suo primo laboratorio nel 1962 in Calle del fumo, il secondo nel 1985 in Calle della mandorla a cui seguirono vari altri negozi e laboratori. Attualmente il suo negozio si trova in Fondamenta Ca' Foscari 3253.

Biography

Paolo Olbi was born in Venice on October 23, 1937. In his youth he renounced a "safe" job as an employee to follow his passion for bookbinding. Self-taught, he opened his first laboratory in 1962 on Calle del Fumo, the second in 1985 on Calle della Mandorla, and subsequently various other shops and laboratories. Currently his store is located on Fondamenta Ca' Foscari 3253.

"Vorrei Parlarti, Signore...."
di Elena Grassi Orsoni

Vorrei parlarti, Signore, della tristezza che appanna la luce dei giorni.
Di questi giorni di una vita senza colori, senza suoni, con mille nomi pesanti
Sul cuore di gente sconosciuta e perduta all'improvviso con la colla solo di appartenere ad un'unica generazione.
Vorrei dire, oltre che pensarlo, che la vita ci ha mostrato la sua crudeltà più feroce
per cui questi tuoi disperati figli presuntuosi, e fino a ieri certi di possedere tutto
nel cavo delle loro mani, si sono ritrovati nudi e smarriti davanti al tempo.
Che cosa puoi suggerire loro, Tu, Signore, perché si affranchino dalla paura e
perché, uscendo dalle loro case improvvisamente vissute in modo sconosciuto, abbiano
il passo sicuro verso il futuro e verso ciò che sarà doveroso compiere?
Qualcuno, seduto ai margini delle ore, aspetta fiducioso che Tu sorrida ad ogni cosa,
all'aria tornata pulita, alle mani tese di un amico da baciare, da accarezzare di nuovo
come si accarezzano i sogni, i ricordi e tutto ciò che nel mondo è buono e non fa male.

"I Would Like to Speak to You, Lord…."
by Elena Grassi Orsoni

I would like to speak to you, Lord, about the sadness that clouds the light of days.
Of these days of a life without colors, without sounds, with a thousand names
that weigh on the hearts of unknown people and are suddenly lost with the only guilt of belonging to a single generation.
I would like to say, besides thinking it, that life has shown us its most ferocious cruelty
for which these desperate, presumptuous children of yours,
until yesterday sure of having everything
in the hollows of their hands,
they have found themselves naked and lost in the face of time.
What can You suggest to them, You, Lord, to free themselves from fear
and because, leaving their homes suddenly lived in an unknown way, they may have
a sure step towards the future
and towards what will be necessary to do?
Someone, sitting on the sidelines of hours, is confidently waiting for You to smile at everything,
to the air that has returned clean, to the outstretched hands of a friend to kiss, to caress again
like caressing dreams, memories and all that in the world is good and harmless.

Biografia

Elena Grassi Orsoni, poetessa veneziana, è nata a Milano il 1 settembre 1931, ma vive a Cannaregio da molto tempo. È la vedova di Ruggero Orsoni, maestro produttore di tessere di mosaico di alta qualità, ancora prodotto a Venezia. Orsoni.com

Biography

Elena Grassi Orsoni, a Venetian poet, was born in Milan on September 1, 1931, but has been living in Cannaregio for a long time. She is the widow of Ruggero Orsoni, master producer of top quality mosaic tiles, still made in Venice. Orsoni.com

"Lettera ad amici dell'altra parte del mondo" di Barbara Pastor

Venezia, luglio 2020

Cari Jennifer e Desmond,
   Come state?
   È da molto che non ci incontriamo a Venezia, da prima che arrivasse l'*Aqua Granda*.
   Sicuramente non avrete perso una parola ne un'immagine di quanto è stato scritto e mostrato di quella notte, anche nel lontano Sud Africa, visto il vostro forte legame con Venezia. E certamente altro tempo passerà prima di poterci vedere di nuovo, dato che la pandemia ci terrà bloccati a lungo.
   Perché scrivere ancora dell'*Aqua Granda*? Sto pensando a quanto le emergenze opposte siano legate: siccità estrema a Cape Town, inondazioni a Venezia. Città vittime del cambiamento climatico.
   E dopo questi fenomeni, decisamente locali, legati a dove e a come le nostre città sono state costruite, è arrivata la pandemia, un evento globale. Abbiamo vissuto in prima persona quello che i vari esperti sanno da tempo: il nostro sistema di vita sul pianeta è insostenibile.
   Mentre leggo sui giornali che siete riusciti a superare la grave crisi di siccità di due anni fa, imparando a far tesoro di ogni goccia d'acqua, che è un'esperienza che poi ti porti dentro per sempre, anche noi qui ci stiamo attrezzando a una nuova quotidianità che temiamo/sappiamo arriverà in autunno.
   Non vorrei che le mie parole suonassero troppo retoriche, ma sono orgogliosa di come noi veneziani siamo riusciti a risollevarci dal disastro, più combattivi di prima. Ma siamo pochi, sempre meno, decimanti dalla speculazione della monocultura turistica. Poco importa se alcuni di noi sono stati complici di questo, non sposta il problema.
   In quella notte di novembre ho sentito quanto la Laguna sia una sostanza primordiale, una grande madre, che dà la vita e la

toglie se non rispettiamo i suoi equilibri. Ho aspettato, smarrita e impotente, che mi invadesse ma il vento (che tanto ha distrutto altrove) mi è stato amico.

La Laguna è il senso di Venezia, la ragione per cui la città è com'è, e la ragione per cui noi veneziani siamo come siamo, indissolubilmente legati all'acqua. Già, grande madre... anche la vostra Romi, ormai veneziana, lo sa molto bene.

Mai come durante il *lockdown* abbiamo potuto constatare lo spopolamento di Venezia. Lo sentivi e lo annusavi, senza vederlo perché eravamo tutti chiusi in casa.

Ho 'rubato' una passeggiata, in aprile, durante un pomeriggio di sole e sono andata fino in Piazza. Mai come in quel giorno la città di pietra mi è apparsa splendida. L'architettura è fatta dagli uomini per gli uomini, ma in quel momento poteva fare a meno di noi.

Sicuramente potrà fare a meno, nel futuro, dell'invasione di gente indifferente.

Venezia e i veneziani hanno sempre saputo ricominciare reinventandosi. Lo faranno anche questa volta, a patto che venga rispettata la sua e la loro diversità.

Con affetto
Barbara

"Letter to Friends on the Other Side of the World" by Barbara Pastor

Venice, July 2020

Dear Jennifer and Desmond,

How are you?

It's been a while since we last met up in Venice: before the *aqua granda*. I'm sure that, with your strong ties with Venice, you followed the reports of the flooding that night even though you were thousands of miles away in South Africa.

It looks like it will be some time before we can meet again, as the pandemic keeps us blocked in our respective countries for who knows how long.

Why am I writing to you about the *aqua granda*? It's because it occurred to me that you suffered the exact opposite in 2018. Extreme drought in Cape Town, flooding in Venice: both cities victims of climate change. Following these decidedly local phenomena—related to where and how our cities were built—we were then all affected by a truly global event, the Covid-19 pandemic. We are experiencing firsthand the results of what the experts have warned us about for some time: that our way of living on this planet is unsustainable.

Two years ago, I read in the papers that you were able to survive the drought by learning to treasure every drop of water—an experience that will stay with you forever. Here, we are also preparing for our "new normal": the recurring flooding that we know will start again in the autumn.

I hope I don't sound too rhetorical, but I am proud of how we Venetians were able to pick ourselves up after the disaster, more determined than before. But there are only a few of us left, and our numbers continue to dwindle due to the monoculture of tourism. It matters little if some of us are complicit in this. It doesn't alter the problem.

More than ever, during that night in November, I realized how much the Lagoon is a primordial, fluid force: like Mother

Nature, it gives life and takes life if we refuse to respect its equilibria. I waited, stunned and powerless, for the water to invade my place, but the wind (that caused great destruction elsewhere) proved to be my friend.

The Lagoon is the reason why Venice is as it is, and the reason why we Venetians are as we are, inextricably linked to the water (as your daughter—who has become a Venetian herself—knows well).

The lockdown made the depopulation of Venice more evident than ever before. You could hear it and feel it, without seeing it because we were all closed in our homes.

On a sunny afternoon in April, I went for a surreptitious walk to Piazza San Marco. Never before had the city of stone appeared so splendid. Architecture is made by people for people, but at that moment it seemed Venice could do without us.

In the future, it will certainly be better off without the processions of tourists, many of whom seem oblivious to its beauty.

Venice and the Venetians have always known how to start over by reinventing themselves. They will do it once again, as long as the specificity of the city and of its residents is respected.

Yours affectionately,
Barbara

Biografia

Barbara Pastor, è architetto. Il suo studio è a piano terra su Rio de la Panada e mentre lavora, sente l'influsso (quasi sempre) benefico dell'acqua.

Biography

Barbara Pastor is an architect with a studio on the ground floor on the Rio de la Panada canal-side. While she is working there, she can feel the (almost always) reassuring presence of the water.

Photograph by Massimo Spada

"Splendor and Sadness"
by Alessandro Santini

The *Aqua Granda*:

My generation grew up with the belief that the world stopped on November 4, 1966. The day of *aqua granda*, the high tide, 1 meter 90 cm, was a lot, too much, and the record has never been repeated.

I don't know how many stories I heard about that day: those stories that your parents, your grandparents always remind you about. The strong *scirocco* wind, the gondolas sunk, the boats in Piazza San Marco, and the incredible few silent videos and photos in black and white with the people rowing everywhere in the city. Those videos have always made me incredibly sad.

The sea had won.

At every high tide, every year, there is always someone who says, "*L'acqua riva sui copi ancuo come nel '66*" ("The water will arrive at the roof today ... as in '66").

Yes, as in '66.

I am a surfer and kite surfer, and the best time for these sports is Autumn. The *scirocco* pushes the sea into this Adriatic angle located in the Venetian Lagoon. The Adriatic Sea is not an ocean, but the *scirocco* storms create very good conditions for the Venetian wave riders. But this also means high tide in the city.

It was a November Tuesday. The forecasts were excellent: 20/25 knots from S/E, the *scirocco* wind, a heavy wind, charged with humidity, the one that you can feel in your bones. The *acqua alta* was expected for that night. Messages had arrived from the tide center: the forecast was 1 m 60 cm, very high, but also the last few days we had had a high tide, just not so high.

I was on the beach, but "Surprise!" It was windy but completely from the other direction—a northeast *bora* wind, the fresh wind, which dries things out. So strange .... But no problem—20 knots and big waves, so I thought, "Let's get on the water." It was a good session, but I expected something better; the forecast was not quite correct, but this can happen.

Maybe also the tide would not be so high, I thought coming home.

After dinner, watching TV, my telephone rang. It was my mother in Venice.

"What's the weather there?" she asked. I live a few kilometers from Venice.

"It's a little windy, mum, and there?"

"There's a strong wind, and the tide is quite high on the *calle*." My mum lives on the top floor where she can see the *calle* from above. The tide hardly ever rose to there, only when it was very high.

"Don't worry, mum, it's the *scirocco* and *acqua alta*. You know it, goodnight."

I checked the phone app called Hi!Tide for the forecast and tide level in real time. It was at 1 m 50 cm, and kept rising.

After one hour my mum called me again.

"Ale, the wind is extremely strong, and the *calle* is full of water."

I took a look out the window, and also at my house the wind was very strong. Looked like a storm.

"Let's check Hi!Tide.... 1 m 70 cm... WHAT?"

And it would continue to rise for another hour. I said to my wife and my kids, "Guys, 1 m 70 cm ... and it keeps on rising ... up to the roof ... as in '66."

The first live video from social networks seemed unreal—there was no difference between a *calle* and a canal. I checked the forecast on Venezia radar: a big storm was at that moment above Venice, 40 knots south wind at the same time as the rising tide, a real disaster, a mix of events that together created a nightmare for the city. As in '66, everything was going the wrong way. I took a look at the San Marco webcam. I couldn't believe it. A lot of videos were showing up on my phone. It was impossible to walk in the streets because of the wind, boats were floating on the Grand Canal out of control, and big waves crashed in front of Piazza San Marco.

I called Lorenzo. We have known each other since we were two years old. We have seen thousands of high tides in our life. He was out of breath and seemed to be running, but in reality he was struggling to slog through the high water. He told me he was going to check the gondola to see if it was still there. "What?" I thought.

He sent me a video.

The gondolas of our mates in front of the Danieli Hotel were on the Riva, mashed at an angle. Two gondolas were inside the hotel, in the reception area.

I couldn't believe it. Close to these *gondole* there was a *vaporetto* on the *fondamenta*, leaning on one side. A water bus on the street? I had to go.

Lorenzo recommended I stay home. I checked Hi!Tide again: 1 m 87 cm.

Noooo, it's not possible. I got dressed and ran out the door. Along the way I thought about my friends—restaurant owners, all the stores and markets. The images and the videos I saw before were fixed in my mind.

Lorenzo called me and told me the storm had passed, and it looked like the tide would start to recede. It was difficult to cross the Ponte della Libertà because the Grand Canal and the bridge seemed to be one thing. In Piazzale Roma it was dark—there was no public lighting. Two taxi boats were on the street. The tide was extremely high. Though I wore very high boots, it was not enough, and the cold water spilled into my boots. The narrow streets were completely dark. At that moment Venice didn't have canals or streets because the water was everywhere. It came inside through the windows of the ground floor. I called my friend and colleague Matteo. He told me in Giudecca was the apocalypse. He saw two *vaporetti* come into the little canals. One had destroyed a bridge. He managed to save his motor boat with a rope, but it was a miracle. A lot of boats broke their moorings and disappeared.

Lorenzo managed to get to Piazza San Marco. He told me that where we work at the gondola station, everything was okay, our gondolas were okay, but it was very dangerous to walk. The tide was rapidly receding, and it left all the debris on the streets.

People had already started cleaning everywhere and got by as best they could ... as in '66.

I took my car and went home. I really struggled to sleep. Had it really happened?

The next day, with the sunlight, we realized what had occurred. When Venice woke up it was seriously injured.

Many water bus stops were terribly damaged, many boats had sunk, ground floors were flooded. The current carried everything. From Sant'Elena to San Marco, the part most affected by the wind, there was not an intact wall. Giudecca's side of the Lagoon was the same. The gondolas in front of the Danieli Hotel were where the tide and the waves had left them, all damaged, alongside a *vaporetto* thrown on the *fondamenta* as if it were a paper boat.

Obviously in the city there was no discussion of anything else, as in '66 ... as in '66. It almost seemed like we got rid of something, but we had something more to offer to the next generation: the colors on the photos and the sounds on the videos.

The Lockdown:

June 3rd, my first day back at work after the lockdown. I covered my gondola very well, and I waited for Matteo, my good buddy, a real brother for me. We have been working together for many years. As often happens, we go towards home together, have a beer or a spritz, some good trash talking, and many laughs. Since Matteo lives on Giudecca, he took the *vaporetto* at the Zattere, we said goodbye, and I continued on to Piazzale Roma.

March 5th, almost three months before, the same thing had happened. Matteo and I had said goodbye. We usually say, "*Ciao fradeo, se vedemo doman*" ("Hi, my brother, see you tomorrow...") but not that day. When will we meet again, bro...? We couldn't say. But we thought it. Oh yes, so sad, we already understood what was happening. In the last days of Carnevale, people and tourists had started to leave the city, and the epidemic was beginning to expand rapidly.

Lockdown.

I could not even imagine empty Venice by day. Many times I have seen empty Venice, silent, but always at night. I have worked many times at night, on commercials, movies shot at night in the dark. Dark Venice is spectacular; the directors know this very well. But what about the day time? At noon on a May day?

Empty, silent, just the sound of the breeze in the *calli*. And the sound of bells can be heard everywhere—they echo in the empty squares.

One Sunday in April I decided to go check on my gondola. The day before it had rained a lot, so I had to go remove the water and clean the boat. In Italy in these days, you could only leave home for work or for reasons considered valid. Only food markets were open, and from Piazzale Roma to San Marco I met only four or five people. I looked at the canals: the water was crystal clear, and the sand and the dark mud of the Lagoon remained in place. Thanks to so few boats passing by, you could see very well the fishes and all the things deposited on the seabed. Many birds, I thought incredulously, had become the real owners of the canals. It's not bad thinking about it—the cormorant is the real king. He is an expert fisherman even when the canals are busy. Passing near the Rio Novo, a canal usually super busy, I saw a family of ducks that climbed the green steps from the canal and passed quietly through the street. I came to Piazza San Marco. It was empty, empty—this means just me and the pigeons. It was about 11 a.m., a sunny day, and when I passed by Florians, everything was closed, the booming sound of my steps under the arcades being the only noise that I heard.

My gondola was there, where I had left it almost a month before on the canal by the San Marco Royal Gardens. It was covered in dust, and there was rain water inside. In an hour I had washed everything. It's a new gondola, only one year old, so after a good wash it looked really beautiful.

I sincerely wanted to row, but the boats were not allowed out in a Venice in lockdown. So I let the desire pass, I saluted the boat with a little sadness, and I left.

I stopped by to see my mother who lives in Cannaregio, at the Campo dei Gesuiti, where I was born. There were more people there. Though you can only go out to buy food or drugs, the Venetians were there—at the greengrocer, in the bakery, in the small supermarkets, all queueing, spaced, with masks and plastic gloves on. One thing that makes you understand that it is a moment of extreme difficulty is that the taverns (*osterie*) were closed. Venice without the *osterie* doesn't make sense. You don't just have a drink in the *osteria*: People go to the *osteria*, drink, talk, spend time with friends, leave and go to another *osteria* ... but not during this period. Mr. Campari and Mr. Aperol were also in lockdown.

Back in early May, with my son Samuel, the oldest of the three, I took him to row, and I wanted to show him Venice in this period. He knows Venice very well. We passed by his school, and there were more people around because the lockdown was less stringent.

Samuel and I arrived in San Marco where we met very few people. He, too, was incredulous and enjoyed Venice's silence. "Let's clean the gondola and go," I said. I at the stern, he at the bow, rowing in the Grand Canal was wonderful during this time. There were very few boats, no waves, and the sweet sound of the boat moving the water seemed to penetrate the open windows of the Venetian palaces.

It's difficult to explain, but there's a mix of feelings in me— the wonder of seeing a beautiful city in all its splendor and the sadness of seeing the biggest hotels closed. They seem abandoned.

After an hour and a half of euphoric rowing, we went back to our canal. I taught Samuel a few maneuvers—he is learning quite well—we covered the boat, and we went home, I happy and more relaxed, he happy and with some extra blisters on his hands.

June 3rd, my first day back at work after the lockdown, I did not convey any customers in my gondola. There are no tourists in Venice. The borders would reopen in two weeks, but many people from all of the Veneto came to Venice for the weekend and guess what ... the *osterie* are open, a great step towards normalcy.

Biography

Alessandro Santini was born in Venice and is a gondolier. He comes from a gondolier family—his father, grandfather, and great-grandfather were all gondoliers. Alessandro is married to Roberta, and they have three kids. He loves traveling, surfing, and playing guitar. Though Alessandro has a desire to live in California, how can he choose? He would miss Venice too much.

"Like a Phoenix"
by Rachele Scarpa

They say, "*per sei ore cresce e per sei ore cala*": for six hours it rises, and for six hours it falls. For many, high water is a fun event, for our guests, and especially for children: we put on *stivali* (boots) and play in the water. For us Venetians, however, the *acqua alta* is always a concern and doesn't conjure up such a joyful image. For six hours the water doesn't always stop rising, and after six hours it doesn't always fall.

While waiting for the arrival of the tidal peak on that evening of November 12, my friends and I gathered for our customary *ombra* (a glass of wine) before dinner, oblivious to the exceptional event that was about to unfold. Suddenly the wind started to intensify, and a large mass of water succeeded in sinking all our certainties, breaking into even the remotest *calli*, *campi*, and *campielli* without asking for permission. Homes on the ground floor had become uninhabitable, and so had shops, artisan workshops, bars, and restaurants. Water filled the *campi* until they resembled lakes, though the lights inside the shops and houses still lit the interiors as on any normal night.

The need to get back on our feet and our determination to return to normal, however, prevailed over despair: we Venetians rolled up our sleeves and discovered not a wounded city, but a stronger, united, and supportive community, and a new opportunity to rethink Venice and rediscover forgotten values.

We hoped we'd never return to the unreal silence and solitude experienced in the days of the *aqua granda*, which was so unlike the normal Venice that everyone knows and loves. Instead, with the same destructive and unexpected force, the Covid-19 crisis came to suffocate again the fragile, newly risen heart of the city.

In some ways, we inhabitants can be considered privileged for having lived during such a unique and, hopefully, unrepeatable period in time: there is no other place where we would have liked to experience the lockdown. We have rediscovered forgotten sounds: the birds, the bells, the splashing of the rowing boats on the canals. The absence of rolling luggage on the previously well-trodden *masegni* (paving stones) and bridges. The silence was unreal. We were witnesses of a new day and of a rediscovered nature. We found a forgotten Venice, now finally OURS.

Venice is often described as a non-place, a theme park, a showcase city in which we Venetians are seen as participants or players in a reality show or period drama. The catastrophic experiences we have lived through meant that like a phoenix, the city of water can rise from its ashes.

Biography

Born and raised on Murano island, Rachele graduated in Communication Studies from the University of Padua. She has a keen interest in the arts, and she has trained as a curator. Passionate about Venice and with a genuine enthusiasm for sharing her knowledge and expertise on all things Venetian with Views on Venice guests from around world, in her spare time Rachele can be found exploring the Lagoon and navigating the "highways and byways" of Venice in her very own boat.

"My Little Dream"
by Giuliano Tonolo

It was a dream come true. I was scrolling through the photos from my phone over and over again, and every time it looked more beautiful. The bright red frame's shape was amazing as well as its eco-ivory leather seats; they seemed so elegant and comfortable! The 9.9 horsepower engine was brand new. On the back of it were striking blue lights. I had just bought a small motorboat, about 15 feet long.

It was the end of September. I have never had a boat before, and I was a little bit worried about it. Would it be easy to drive? And park? I used to drive my car—I thought—and I have had a driver's license for many years, so why shouldn't it be the same? Of course it is not the same, I thought. A boat is a boat, a car is a car!

That day I decided to bring with me Carlotta, the nice young coach who is teaching me to row. She knows well how to drive a motorboat. We jumped for the first time into this red floating box and left the little pier on the Grand Canal where it had been moored. It was so exciting to touch the steering wheel for the first time! The day was sunny and the Lagoon breeze light and sweet. Carlotta almost didn't say a word during our journey: "I am probably not driving so badly," I thought, satisfied. After crossing the Giudecca Canal, the part of the Lagoon that divides Venice from the Island of Giudecca, we finally parked at the dockyard. Unfortunately, the space I had rented was not in the first row but about 15 or more feet away from the shore. There was not a pier to connect the space to the shore, so we had to wait for someone who would be passing through there to ask for a ride. It was the only big inconvenience of that place. At the beginning it was not easy to measure for parking and learn how to tie the ropes to the poles. I was lucky to have Carlotta with me! And I am not embarrassed to say that she did most of the work that day!

Since that day I had no other opportunity to drive my boat. On the 12th of November I stayed at home all day. The *acqua alta* didn't permit me to get out, not even for a short walk with my dog due to his physical needs. When dark had fallen, the sound of the wind was so loud echoing inside all the rooms of my house. I still have impressed in my mind the terrible sound of the shutters banging on the outside wall. It is a familiar sound; I had heard it several times during the *acqua alta* in the past, but every time it disturbs me in the same way. It disturbs me like the siren sound that announces every time the arrival of a new flood. They both move something inside of me. I watched the news and realized that probably there would be major flooding in Venice that night, but I hadn't realized how serious it was going to be. I was worried about my boat, but I forced myself to not think about it.

The next morning the tide was still so high to dissuade me to face reality. I was really nervous and restless. After noon I gathered the courage to go outside. I put on my boots and went to the place where the boat was moored. I was shocked when from afar I wasn't able to see the bright red frame.

Okay—I thought—the boat is gone! She probably untied herself from the poles and went offshore! But soon I changed my mind: peeking out of the water was the orange plastic fuel tank that was floating close to the poles. "Oh my gosh, the boat is at the bottom of the canal, for sure!" I thought. Immediately I felt myself become so sad and resigned. "I can't believe it. I have just bought it, and I drove it just twice!" I said out loud.

I decided to go back home, waiting for the water level to go down. The surprise came soon. A few hours later the red bow of the boat emerged from the water like the tip of an iceberg. In that moment I realized what had happened and that I needed someone to help me to get it out. I called the Venice fire fighters, but they were too busy to come. Many boats like mine or bigger had sunk or disappeared somewhere in those tragic hours.

I called a private boatman, and he came the next day. He had to use a crane to pull it out of the water. He brought it to the shipyard on the island. One month later the boat was ready. I learned that if the engine remains under water for a long time, the salt can damage the electrical and mechanical parts. Once out of the water, they have a short time period to wash every single part of it with sweet water. Fortunately, I was able to save the engine. I had to change all the electrical parts, including the battery. I lost my new precious ivory leather seats in the bottom of the canal. The boat was completely repaired after one month, so I took it away.

I parked it at the same place because at that time I didn't have another option. I was worried that a new high tide would come.

Unbelievably, in December another *acqua alta* submerged my little treasure for the second time! While I am writing this in July, it is still at the shipyard being fixed.

I pray every day it will be ready before this summer ends. I have decided to move the boat to another place where it will be safer, a place close to the shore that I can easily get to every time. I would like to use it as the Venetians do. They used to go to the "*bàcan*," thin strips of sands situated near to the *bocche di porto*, the harbor mouth. These strips of sand emerge from the water only during the low tide, and they disappear when the tide rises. It is a tradition for Venetians to sunbathe or dive into the water, and it has created the common expression "*andare in bacàn*," which means "Let's go to the *bacàn*."

Talking with people that own boats, they ask me, "Why doesn't your boat have a name? Boats need to have a name!" Probably they are right. Probably I was so unlucky because I haven't given her a name yet!

What kind of name should I give to my boat? Suggestions are welcome!

Biography

My name is Giuliano. I was born in Mirano, a nice town located in the Venetian countryside. I moved to Venice more than ten years ago, most of this time staying in Giudecca. Usually the Venetians leave the old town and move to the mainland; I believe I am one of the few who did the opposite. I've chosen Venice because I love to live here. I like acting and writing and being surprised by life every day. Please send me your suggestions about the boat name at the following address: tonolo.giuliano@gmail.com.

Acknowledgments

I am ever grateful to the many people who have helped bring this book to completion. Their expertise fills so many gaps in my own abilities and knowledge or helps to connect me with others. Thank you in particular to Tiziana Businaro, Graziella Giusto, Michelle Miller, and Philip August for translation help, as well as the help offered by so many of the contributors to this book. Graziella also went above and beyond to procure a mask for her front cover photo. Greg Mohr connected me with some fabulous storytellers. Paolo Olbi's apprentices, Anna and Elena, aided in communications and many small details, as likewise did Kasia Ruszkowska as we communicated with We are here Venice. Once again, Iris Loredana offered invaluable advice for the book cover. Continued thanks go to my friends Karen and David Koppett, Laura Rice, Heather Jones, Amy Payne, Diane Lanctot, and Marco Zecchin for their unfailing advice and encouragement. More spritz in the backyard, please!

Of course, this book is the brainchild of Rosemary Wilmot, my friend across the pond. Rosemary provided the initial idea for *Venice Rising*, but then she became a tireless advocate, helping to move the project forward daily. Though we had first met online through social media, our collaboration and friendship developed into a beautiful partnership. She brought in many of our contributors, who brought in more contributors, always increasing the excitement for the book. Rosemary has a gift for communicating and bringing people together, and she shared that gift with me, making my work lighter and more fun. This book wouldn't exist without her. *Grazie mille*!

None of my books could exist without the constant feedback, guidance, moral support, advice, and technical savvy of my partner of 18 years, RJ Wofford II. During the creation of this book, during a pandemic, we got married! Now that's love, and I'm grateful daily to have him in my life.

About the Editor

Kathleen Ann González has written and published with various periodicals, three anthologies, and a textbook. She has independently-published five books: *A Beautiful Woman in Venice*, *Seductive Venice: In Casanova's Footsteps*, *Free Gondola Ride*, *A Small Candle*, and *First Spritz Is Free*. Supernova Edizioni publishes her books in Italy, including the translation into Italian of *Casanova's Venice: A Walking Guide*. She also organized the symposium "Casanova in Place," bringing together Casanova scholars in Venice in 2019. As a high school English teacher, Kathleen Ann González has won various awards and recognition for her work. Passionate about travel, González finds any excuse to hop on an airplane, particularly to Venice.

Visit KathleenAnnGonzalez.com or follow her blog at seductivevenice.wordpress.com.

Manufactured by Amazon.ca
Bolton, ON